Real Options and Investment Incentives

Gunther Friedl

Real Options and Investment Incentives

Springer

Professor Dr. Gunther Friedl
Johannes Gutenberg University of Mainz
Jakob-Welder-Weg 9
D-55099 Mainz
Germany
gunther.friedl@uni-mainz.de

Library of Congress Control Number: 2006936839

ISBN-10 3-540-48266-0 Springer Berlin Heidelberg New York
ISBN-13 978-3-540-48266-6 Springer Berlin Heidelberg New York

Springer is part of Springer Science+Business Media

springer.com

Production: LE-TeX Jelonek, Schmidt & Vöckler GbR, Leipzig
Cover-design: Erich Kirchner, Heidelberg

SPIN 11916116 88/3100YL - 5 4 3 2 1 0 Printed on acid-free paper

Foreword

Capital rationing and compensation are the most important instruments to control managers in divisionalized firm. Therefore performance-based compensation plays a prominent role in modern managerial accounting research. As shareholder value and performance measures like Economic Value Added as well as stock options are used in many companies all over the world performance-based incentive systems became important for practice, too.

This book is very innovative as it connects real options with incentive theory. The author analyzes how incentive systems have to be structured if managers have to decide on investments sequentially under uncertainty. Mathematical models are solved on growth options, switching options and waiting options as they arise in decisions on research and development, flexible manufacturing systems and the postponement of investments. Two types of models are used and exemplified very clear in their characteristics and their differences, principal agent models and goal congruence models.

Using their specific properties in order to analyze performance-based incentive and capital rationing systems for sequential investments this book provides very interesting new results. On the one hand it gives scientific explanations on empirical investment processes and empirical hypotheses to be tested. On the other hand it yields valuable information on the structuring of incentive and capital rationing systems in practice.

This book demonstrates how modern accounting theory can be developed. In connecting different concepts like investment, real option and incentive theory important new results can be found. They increase our theoretical knowledge and give useful insights for the decision making in firms and the structuring of their controlling systems. In sum, this book takes an important step in managerial accounting research towards a better understanding of investment incentives. Therefore, it will prove useful both to researchers in this area as well as firms.

Munich, August 2006 *Prof. Dr. Dr. h.c. Hans-Ulrich Küpper*

Acknowledgments

This monograph was accepted as a post-doctoral thesis by the Munich School of Management of the Ludwig-Maximilians-Universität Munich. I am indebted to many people for their ideas, support, and encouragement.

I would like to express my gratitude to my post-doctoral supervisor, Prof. Dr. Dr. h.c. Hans-Ulrich Küpper, whose expertise, understanding, and support added considerably to my work. He was always willing to discuss ideas and he created a highly stimulating atmosphere at his Institute of Operations Management and Managerial Accounting. I would like to thank the other member of my committee, Prof. Dr. Bernd Rudolph, for the assistance he provided at all levels of the research project.

Large parts of this work benefited from the many discussions during a stay at the Graduate School of Business at Stanford University. A very special thank goes to Prof. Dr. Stefan Reichelstein, who invited me to spend more than half a year at Stanford. He spent a lot of time discussing ideas and much of my work has been heavily influenced by these discussions. I also appreciate the many valuable comments of the participants of the accounting seminar at Stanford University, where I presented parts of this work.

I benefited greatly from my many colleagues at the Munich School of Management. Dr. Nils Balke provided detailed comments to parts of this work. Prof. Dr. Burkhard Pedell and Dr. Rouven Bergmann not only have been partners and co-authors in our joint projects, they also became good friends. Thanks also go to Dr. Markus Deliano, Wolfgang Götz, Dr. Christian Hilz, and Dr. Alexander Susanek to name just a few of my former colleagues.

Vauable Comments and suggestions have also been provided by Prof. Dr. Robert Göx, Prof. Dr. Thomas Pfeiffer, Prof. Dr. Barbara Pirchegger, Prof. Dr. Madhav Rajan, participants at the MAS conference of the AAA in Miami, the EAA conference in Seville, the Accounting Research Workshop in Stuttgart, the GEABA-symposium in Frankfurt/Main, the GOR conference in Heidelberg, and seminars at the universities of Magdeburg and Witten-Herdecke. Financial support by the DFG is also gratefully acknowledged.

I thank Katharina Wetzel-Vandai, together with the people at Springer, for her dedication and patience during all stages of publishing this work.

Finally, I dearly thank my parents for the support they provided me through my entire life. I must give immense thanks to my wife Carolin and our children Anna, Sebastian, and Florian (who was born after finishing this work). Their love and support were of immeasurable value to me.

Mainz, October 2006 *Prof. Dr. Gunther Friedl*

Contents

List of Abbreviations

CVA	Cash Value Added
ed.	edition
et seqq.	and the following
EVA	Economic Value Added
Fig.	Figure
R&D	Research and Development
RoI	Return on Investment
SFAS	Statement of Financial Accounting Standards
U.S.	United States (of America)
US-GAAP	United States-Generally Accepted Accounting Principles
WACC	weighted-average cost of capital
ZfB	Zeitschrift für Betriebswirtschaft
zfbf	Zeitschrift für betriebswirtschaftliche Forschung

1

Introduction

Many large corporations delegate investment decision-making authority to their divisions.[1] Not headquarters but rather divisional managers are frequently responsible even for major investment decisions. Delegation has important advantages including the fact that divisional managers are usually better informed about the product market they are responsible for.[2] Hence in principle, they should be able to make better decisions from a company's perspective, i.e., they should be able to maximize the value of the company by making the right decision.

However, divisional managers are usually not machines acting automatically in the best interest of the company's owners. They rather are human beings who are more likely to maximize their own utility instead of objectives imposed by an organization. Therefore, delegating decision-making to better informed managers means that these managers have room to pursue their own objectives, possibly different to those of the company. In this case, the company has to use instruments to align the manager's objectives with those of the company's owners. In case of full delegation of investment decision-making authority, the manager should have an incentive to make exactly the same decision, headquarters would make had it the same information as the better informed manager. If headquarters wants to use the manager's information for making a decision on its own, it has to design an instrument that ensures truthful reporting of the manager's information to headquarters. In this case, only information gathering is delegated but investment decision-making is centralized.

[1] A survey by Reece & Cool (1982) among large U.S. firms indicates that almost three quarter of the responding firms delegate decision-making authority to investment centers.

[2] See, Milgrom & Roberts (1992), pp. 544-545.

There is a whole variety of instruments that ensures either truthful reporting of information, which is available decentrally or helps to align the interests of divisional managers and their companies. Each of these instruments makes some assumptions regarding its effects on human motivation and behavior. A basic distinction on a person's motivation within companies is whether it is intrinsic or extrinsic.[3] For intrinsic motivated managers, external rewards only play a minor role. It is less important to give these persons incentives in order to ensure that they choose the right action choices. For extrinsic motivated managers, the prospect of external rewards such as performance-based compensation is a source of motivation. They have to be given incentives to align their interests with those of the company. In line with much of the economic literature on incentives within organizations, in this work I restrict myself on the case when managers are extrinsic motivated and pursue different objectives than the company. Of course, I do not question the importance of analyzing reasons and effects of intrinsic motivation. However, in my view the significance of extrinsic motivation justifies a separated analysis.[4]

The literature has extensively analyzed the case of delegated investment decision-making when a divisional manager is better informed about the profitability of investment projects than headquarters. Similarly to this work, the focus at least of the economic analyses has been on incentive instruments, which address the extrinsic motivation of managers. However, most of this literature has taken a very simple view of corporate investment decisions. It usually considers investment projects as a single yes-or-no-decision with a certain or uncertain outcome.[5] Once the investment decision has been made, there is no room for additional subsequent decisions. Clearly, this view is a considerable simplification of reality, where many projects require subsequent decisions. In research and development investments, for example, after the initial investment decision has been made, it is necessary to decide whether the project should be continued or not. A factory that has been built for different product lines requires subsequent decisions on the kind of product line to be produced. Within the investment valuation literature, this prop-

---

[3] See Neuberger (1980), p. 1361.

[4] For an experimental study analyzing the importance of intrinsic and extrinsic motivation in a capital budgeting setting see Butler, et al. (2002). The interaction between intrinsic and extrinsic motivation is discussed by Kreps (1997) and formally analyzed by Benabou & Tirole (2002).

[5] Frequently, the literature assumes a continuum of investment levels, where the single yes-or-no-decision is substituted by a decision on the exact level of investment expenditures out of a continuum of possible choices.

erty of investment decisions has been thoroughly analyzed. Corporate finance textbooks offer a variety of solutions to such valuation problems in a single-person decision context.[6]

The objective of this work is to analyze the problem of delegated decision-making within firms, when investment projects are characterized by the possibility to make subsequent decisions after the initial investment decision has been made. To put it slightly differently, this work takes a dynamic perspective on investment decision-making under uncertainty, when information is asymmetrically distributed. The importance of such a perspective has been emphasized by various authors, but up to now the academic literature has not said much about this problem from a theoretical standpoint. Neither the investment valuation literature nor the literature on controlling investment decisions has tried to close this gap between the complexity of reality and its transformation into economic modelling.

Since different types of investment projects frequently involve completely different information and decision structures with very specific properties, this work's approach is to analyze the problem described above for specific and well defined situations. Although a more general and comprehensive approach seems to be desirable, a careful modelling of specific facets of the investment decision-making situation is required in order to derive meaningful insights and possible recommendations for corporate practice. I therefore start in chapter 2 with a comprehensive review of the institutional and methodological background for the analysis of investment incentives. Important properties of investment decisions are classified in order to confine the object of investigation. I discuss various instruments for controlling investment decisions, restricting attention in particular to capital rationing and performance-based compensation. I finally discuss advantages and disadvantages of competing theoretical methodologies that are in principle able to address the problem of incentive issues for complex investment decisions. Since principal-agent models as well as goal congruence models have their specific benefits and downsides, the following analysis uses both of them to fully exploit the range of potential statements to the kind of investment incentive problems under consideration.

Chapter 3 analyzes capital budgeting for research and development decisions that have the form of a growth option. The arrival of new information on the profitability of the project is crucial for the decision whether to go ahead with the project or abandon it. When the manager has a preference for organizational slack, the analysis demonstrates the

[6] See, e.g., Brealey & Myers (1996), pp. 255-264 and pp. 589-616.

occurrence of capital rationing, i.e. not all projects with positive net present value are undertaken. The extent of rationing strongly depends on the manager's participation constraints, which can be interpreted as a form of the organizational arrangement. Furthermore, the analysis shows the optimality of a staged budgeting procedure, which is indeed observable in corporate practice for budgeting procedures in the area of research and development. In this chapter, a dynamic principal-agent model is used to derive the described results. This kind of model buys propositions on optimal contracts between headquarters and the manager at the price of high mathematical complexity. Therefore I continue the analysis by restricting myself to certain types of contracts by using models of goal congruence in the subsequent chapters.

Chapter 4 focuses on the analysis of residual income as a performance measure for investments in flexible manufacturing systems when investment decision-making is decentralized. Flexible manufacturing systems are characterized by the option to adjust either the system's input or output goods in order to take advantage of current developments like for example demand or prices. This valuable switching option is usually not recognized by a standard design of the residual income performance measure. Indeed, the analysis shows the occurrence of underinvestment, when residual income is used in a standard way. However, I also propose some adjustments for the residual income measure in the presence of switching options, which achieve goal congruence for the selection of investment projects.

A similar idea is used in chapter 5 to analyze the incentive properties of residual income as a performance measure, when investment can be postponed, or, in the language of the real options literature, when there is a valuable waiting option. The analysis demonstrates the problems of the existing performance measures. In particular, divisional managers will invest to early, if the performance measure is not adjusted for the waiting option. However, a simple adjustment of the capitalization rules can achieve goal congruence between headquarters and the divisional manager. Furthermore, I demonstrate that the existence of hurdle rates which are higher than the cost of capital can improve the investment behavior of managers from headquarters' perspective. This result is remarkable, since it corresponds to an empirically observable phenomenon, which has been traditionally explained by managerial private information.

Chapter 6 concludes by presenting some remarks on the contribution of this work to the existing literature. Limitations of the models in this work and its assumptions as well as empirical implications are discussed.

I finally provide some ideas for extensions of these models and further research.

2

Institutional and Methodological Background for the Analysis of Investment Incentives

2.1 Investment Decision Making Within Divisionalized Firms

2.1.1 General Properties of Capital Investment Decisions

The analysis of incentive problems for capital investment decisions has to be specific of the types and properties of investment decisions under consideration, since the term investment can be defined quite broadly and its meaning is sometimes fairly diffuse. To define the scope of this work, the following classification of important characteristics of capital investment decisions, as illustrated in table 2.1, is helpful.

First, and most importantly, cash flows resulting from investment decisions can be uncertain or not. Real-life investment decisions have to deal virtually exclusively with uncertainty. It is difficult, if not impossible, to find an example for an investment decision with certain cash flows.[1] Uncertainty can affect both the initial investment outlay as well as cash flows from operations. Frequently, uncertainty is more important for cash flows that appear far in the future than cash flows that are promptly following the initial investment decision.

The second characteristic considers the question, if an initial investment decision comprises the possibility to make a subsequent decision. For example, building a factory allows for the subsequent decision of mothballing or abandoning operations. Clearly, if there is no uncertainty, there is no need for making a subsequent investment decision,

[1] The valuation literature on investments as well as whole companies has extensively analyzed problems under uncertainty. For textbook treatments see, e.g., Luenberger (1998), pp. 137-474; Copeland & Weston (1988), pp. 77-355; Brealey & Myers (1996), pp. 141-314; Franke & Hax (1999), pp. 287-354; Damodaran (2002).

since all necessary decisions can be made instantly. However, the arrival of new information can lead to a consecutive investment decision that is only available, if the initial investment decision has been made.[2]

Table 2.1. Important characteristics of capital investment decisions

Characteristic	**Specification**
Uncertainty of cash flows	yes | no
Consecutive decision possible	yes | no
Level of decision making	centrally | decentrally
Distribution of information	symmetrically | asymmetrically

A third facet of capital investment decisions is, whether they are made by a central headquarters or by decentral divisions, which are responsible only for part of the company's operations. In small companies, major investment decisions are usually made by the executive board, i.e. centrally. In contrast, large companies often delegate decision rights to the better informed divisions of the company and let them decide on investments decentrally.[3]

The last characteristic refers to the distribution of information among decision-makers. When at least two decision makers for capital investment decisions are present, which is true in the case of decentralized companies, two cases have to be distinguished. Both parties can either be symmetrically informed, meaning that they have the same decision-relevant information. The more realistic case, though, assumes, that one party is better informed than the other. This is the case of asymmetrically distributed information.

This work focuses on the case, when investment decisions are characterized by

- a high degree of cash flow uncertainty,
- the possibility to make subsequent decisions,
- decentral decision making or information gathering, and
- asymmetrically distributed information.

[2] For these and further examples of subsequent decision making see, e.g. Brealey & Myers (1996), pp. 255-264; Damodaran (2002), pp. 772-816.

[3] Of course, there is no general rule how the distribution of investment decision rights depends on the size of a company. Even in some very large divisionalized companies, approval of major investment decisions by the board of directors is required. This can be seen as a mixed system of a combined central and decentral decision-making, which is quite common in corporate practice. See Stanley & Block (1984); Petty, et al. (1975).

This combination of properties for capital investment decisions is particularly meaningful for major investments in large decentralized companies. But it is certainly not restricted to this situation, since, e.g., minor investment projects can also be subject to a considerable amount of uncertainty. Therefore, this work is relevant for a huge class of situations.

Taking the net present value rule as a starting point, previous work on capital investments has usually taken one of two views, as illustrated in table 2.2. On the one hand, the net present value rule has been extended to situations with uncertainty and managerial flexibility, which includes the possibility to react to new information. There are two major lines of literature analyzing this point. One is the literature on decision tree analysis, starting in the sixties of the last century.[4] The other line of literature has become popular under the term 'real options' and started in the late seventies of the last century.[5] While this literature has examined the valuation of investment opportunities under uncertainty and managerial flexibility very thoroughly, it has almost entirely focused on a single-person decision context. Decentral investment decision making and asymmetrically distributed information has not been considered in these types of models.

Table 2.2. Lines of literature on controlling and valuing investment decisions

Controlling Investment Decisions	Valuing Investment Projects	
	without flexibility	with flexiblity
Central investment decisions or symmetric information	Net present value rule	Decision tree analysis Real option valuation
Decentral investment decisions and asymmetric information	Agency models Goal congruence models	

On the other hand, this last aspect has been comprehensively analyzed in the managerial accounting and financial economics literature,

---

4 See Magee (1964); Wilson (1969); Laux (1971); Hax & Laux (1972).

5 This idea has been expressed in Myers (1977) and relies on methods that have initially been developed and used for the valuation of financial options (Black & Scholes (1973); Merton (1973)). For an extensive review of this literature see Dixit & Pindyck (1994); Trigeorgis (1996).

mainly on the basis of agency models.[6] Another line of literature used a simpler environment than an optimal contracting setting to derive results for investment incentives under asymmetric information, namely goal congruence models.[7] However, in both lines of literature, the investment decision usually is modelled as a single simple investment decision.[8] There is no possibility to make a subsequent decision, if the uncertain environment evolves in a certain direction. Somehow surprisingly, a lack of work can be found on a combination of these aspects,[9] despite its obvious practical importance, and although various authors have proposed research in this area.[10] Only recently, researchers have started to address specific problems of a combination of real options and investment incentive issues.[11] The following examples may help to illustrate the relevance of the kind of investment problem under consideration.

Research and Development (R&D) A typical example for investments with not only the opportunity but also the need of making subsequent decisions are investments in research and development. If the first results of a research project are promising, the company might want to go ahead with the project and develop a new product. If they are not, the company might want to abandon the project. A decentral R&D decision making units might have objectives that are different from those of headquarters, which can include more funding than which is actually

---

[6] For comprehensive reviews of different aspects of this literature see, e.g., Lambert (2001); Antle & Fellingham (1997); Gibbons (1998).

[7] See Rogerson (1997) and Reichelstein (1997). Dutta & Reichelstein (2002a) summarize results of this literature for a variety of business transactions.

[8] See, e.g., the models by Rogerson (1997); Reichelstein (1997); Reichelstein (2000); Antle & Eppen (1985); Zhang (1997); Bernardo, et al. (2001); Harris & Raviv (1996); Harris & Raviv (1998).

[9] Textbook treatments of these topics also follow this classification. The valuation problems are treated mainly in corporate finance or valuation textbooks without taking the view of decentral decision making within organizations. See, e.g., Brealey & Myers (1996); Copeland & Weston (1988); Luenberger (1998); Schmidt (1990). On the other hand, problems of decentral decision making are described mainly in textbooks on managerial accounting. Here however, more complex investment structures are completely neglected. See, e.g., Ewert & Wagenhofer (2003); Hansen & Mowen (2000); Horngren & Foster (1991); Küpper (2001).

[10] See, e.g., Brennan & Trigeorgis (2000); Bromwich & Walker (1998); Trigeorgis (1996).

[11] Recent work includes Antle, et al. (2000); Antle, et al. (2001); Arya & Glover (2001); Arya, et al. (2001); Arya & Glover (2002); Crasselt (2003a); Crasselt (2003b); Dutta (2001); Grenadier & Wang (2003); Mittendorf (2003).

necessary to successfully complete the project or a deep desire to go for the technically rather than the economically best solution.

Investing in a Flexible Manufacturing System Another example of a combined complex valuation and incentive problem is the decision to invest in a new flexible manufacturing system. The advantage of such a system compared to a traditional system is its capability to produce different products if the demand for the originally produced product vanishes. Its disadvantage is the higher investment cost. If a decentral decision maker has to decide upon investment, a possible incentive problem that might arise, is that the manager might possibly leave the firm, before the value of a flexible manufacturing system, namely the option to switch to an alternative output materializes. He therefore might wrongly decide to invest in a traditional system.

Investing in Capacity A third example of these kinds of problems is the decision to invest in additional capacity. In many cases, this decision can be made today, to fully meet the present demand, or later, to wait and see, how the uncertain demand really evolves. If the decision maker has a waiting option, but also a shorter time horizon within the firm, he might invest immediately into additional capacity in order to realize benefits, although waiting could have been the better choice from a company's perspective.

These three examples are chosen to illustrate the problem when the arrival of new information allows for a new decision in the presence of incentive problems. Various comprehensive classifications of possible real options in capital investment decisions with further examples, but without considering incentive problems can be found in the real options literature.[12]

2.1.2 Decentralization, Asymmetric Information, and Its Consequences for Incentive Problems

One of the basic presumptions of this work is that investment decision-making is decentralized, i.e., decision-making authority is delegated to the lower levels of a company like, e.g., divisions. There are various reasons for decentralization, including:[13]

Gathering and Using Local Information Decentral managers are often better informed about their markets and investment opportunities in these markets than central management.

---

[12] See, e.g., Trigeorgis (1996), pp. 2-3; Amram & Kulatilaka (1999), pp. 10-11; Friedl (2000), p. 23.

[13] See Hansen & Mowen (2000); pp. 518-519.

Focusing of Central Management Delegating investment decisions allows central management to spend more time on important strategic decisions.

Training and Motivating Segment Managers Many large companies use decentralization as a motivational device for their junior management. They get responsibilities relatively early in their careers and this also trains them to be able to take higher level jobs within the company.

Enhanced Competition by Exposing Segments to Market Forces By decentralizing investment decisions and keeping track of the results, each division's performance can be evaluated and compared to the results of other divisions within the company.

These advantages of decentralizing decision-making are encountered by some difficulties that are a result of dissecting the interdependencies[14] between the central decision unit and their decentral counterparts. Possible problems of decentralizing include[15]

Defining Divisions and Reporting Relationships There are various dimensions, divisions could be structured, including products, customers, functions, and geographic dimensions. The right structure and size as well as the right reporting relationships between the divisions and central management depends on many influencing factors and can be easily chosen wrongly.

Assigning Activities and Responsibility to Levels The extent to which decentralization should take place depends on the answer to the question, if the gains from delegating a specific function outweighs possible economies of scale by keeping it centralized.

The Transfer Pricing Problem If different divisions exchange their goods, a price must be set to compensate the divisions for delivery. Despite ongoing research in this area[16], for many situations it is still not clear how to determine the right price.

Incentive and Control Issues If the decentral decision unit follows objectives that are different from the objectives of central management, some kinds of incentive mechanisms have to be installed, which ensure an alignment of interests.

Depending on the extent to which responsibilities are delegated to decentral units, various types of divisions or responsibility centers can be distinguished.[17] While in cost centers managers are only responsible for

[14] For a classification of possible interdependencies see Küpper (2001), pp. 32-34.

[15] See Milgrom & Roberts (1992), pp. 546-552.

[16] See, e.g., Baldenius & Reichelstein (2002); Baldenius, et al. (2002); Anctil & Dutta (1999); Göx (2000); Pfeiffer (2002). For an overview, see Wagenhofer (2002).

[17] See, e.g., Küpper (2001), pp. 309-312; Hansen & Mowen (2000), pp. 516-517.

the input side,[18] i.e. costs, in revenue centers the managers hold responsibility only for the output side, i.e. sales. Profit centers are measured in terms of annually profits and therefore combine cost and revenue responsibilities on a periodic basis. The highest degree of responsibility can be found in investment centers, where managers decide on capital investments and are responsible for long-term success.[19]

This work does not aim on determining the right degree of delegation.[20] I rather take as given a certain form of delegation or centralization of investment decision rights, neglecting problems like defining divisions and assigning activities to divisions. Depending on the type of problem, I analyze capital budgeting procedures where investment profitabilities have to be reported to central management as well as a completely delegated decision making of investment centers, both in the context of the arrival of new information and managerial flexibility. I therefore focus on incentive problems and control issues between central management and investment centers with different degrees of investment responsibilities.[21]

2.1.3 Types of Incentive Problems for Corporate Investment Decisions

Delegating decision making authority to managers of investment centers leads to a number of incentive problems. They can be distinguished between incentive problems with respect to investment decisions and incentive problems with respect to operational decisions. While investment incentive problems deal with the selection and the decisions for investment projects, operational incentive problems consider the problem of incentives for cost-reducing or revenue-enhancing activities.

---

[18] Ewert & Wagenhofer (2003), pp. 459 make an additional distinction for responsibility centers with respect to the input side by distinguishing cost centers and expense centers.

[19] A survey by Reece & Cool (1982) yielded the result that from a sample of 620 of the largest American companies 74% have at least two investment centers. It is not entirely clear, though, if the definition of investment center in this survey was the same as in this work.

[20] See Melumad & Reichelstein (1987). For a model analyzing this question in the context of capital investment decision rights, see Baiman & Rajan (1995).

[21] Additional incentive problems might arise between shareholders and central management (see, e.g., Jensen & Meckling (1976); Fama (1980); Fama & Jensen (1983)) as well as between divisional managers and the divisional employees.

In recent years, a growing number of papers has been considering combined operational and investment incentive problems.[22] An advantage of this combined treatment is that possible interdependencies between both problems enter the analysis. The main motivation for it is the assumption, that the manager is not only responsible for investment decision-making, but also for all kinds of operational decisions. While this might be true for managers of relatively small divisions or for divisions, where the manager's decision-making authority is limited to small investments, in large divisions, the divisional top management has only little to do with operational decisions. The divisional top management is concerned with major investment decisions, while operational decisions are delegated to lower levels. In this case, a separation of the analysis of investment incentive problems from operational incentive problems seems to be a reasonable modelling choice. Moreover, this kind of separation allows for a modelling of more specific aspects of the isolated incentive problems, like, for example, a more realistic modelling of the investment project. Since this work focuses on incentive problems for complex investment projects, the analysis will not consider incentive problems on operational decisions in order to isolate investment-specific incentive effects.[23]

Despite this restriction, some different types of investment incentive problems can be distinguished and are well known in literature. The first incentive problem arises due to asymmetric information between headquarters and the divisional manager on specific properties of the investment. The divisional manager might be better informed about the investment cost, or the revenues generated by the investment decision, or both of them. An incentive problem arises, if the manager can use his informational advantage to increase his utility at the expense of central management. For example, the manager might overstate the investment costs to receive excessive budgets. These excessive budgets can be used by buying better equipment than what is really needed or shifting money to nonprofitable projects. The described problem is of the adverse selection or hidden information type.[24]

The second incentive problem has to do with the managerial time horizon. For operational incentive problems, the managerial time horizon does not play any role, if the consequences of the actions are reflected in the results almost immediately. However investments are char-

[22] See, e.g., Dutta & Reichelstein (2002b); Dutta & Reichelstein (2002c); Hofmann (2001), pp. 141-179.

[23] See also the discussion in section 2.3.2.

[24] Antle & Fellingham (1997) provide a comprehensive review of this literature.

acterized by the fact that the investment benefits are temporally decoupled from the investment decision. Then the company's time horizon and the manager's time horizon might come apart. Usually, the managerial time horizon is shorter than the time horizon of the company or its shareholders.[25] Possible reasons for this hypothesis include the chance that the manager leaves the firm or at least his position within the firm before all benefits of the investment have been realized. In this case, it is difficult to make him responsible for possible bad outcomes.

The third incentive problem arises before the ultimate investment decision. Before deciding for a specific investment project, the manager must incur personally costly effort to find a profitable project. The more effort the manager spends, the more information he gets about the exact profitability of an investment project.[26] The subsequent investment decision is based on the information produced by the manager.[27] This incentive problem can be regarded as moral hazard. It arises because of unobservable managerial effort, which has consequences for the success of investment decision making. Despite its relevance for specific situations, for lack of space I do not cover this type of incentive problems in this work, but only the first and the second.

2.2 Instruments for Controlling Capital Investment Decisions

2.2.1 Classifying Instruments for Controlling Investment Decisions

Controlling investment decisions requires instruments that coordinate the activities of central management with the decentral divisional managers. According to *Küpper*[28], the following comprehensive[29] coordination systems can be distinguished:

Central Management Systems In central management systems, decision rights and the right to issue instructions to subordinates are widely centralized. The coordination of all action choices is ensured by central directives.

---

[25] See Dutta & Reichelstein (2002a); Laux (1999), pp. 285-316; Pfaff (1998); Pfeiffer (2003); Reichelstein (1997); Rogerson (1997).

[26] See Schiller (2001).

[27] See also Lambert (1986).

[28] See Küpper (2001), pp. 313-406.

[29] The coordination mechanisms are comprehensive in the sense that they address not only a single but a whole variety of problems of leadership and its coordination within firms.

Budgeting Budgets allow decision makers to move with their actions within certain boundaries, determined by the budget. The degree of delegation depends on the precision with which central management specifies the tasks that have to be fulfilled. In capital budgeting, the allocation of resources comes along with the implementation of a specific project.

Performance Measurement Systems Performance measurement systems define and monitor mostly quantitative performance targets. They serve as a vertical as well as horizontal coordination instrument, since they break down general objectives of a company to the divisional level and even lower levels.

Transfer Pricing The exchange of goods between autonomous divisions as well as between central management and the divisions can be coordinated by transfer prices. This instrument presumes a largely decentralized company.

Obviously, the relevance of central management systems as a coordination instrument is limited in my setting, because I explicitly consider the case of asymmetrically distributed information with the need for delegated decision making, or, alternatively, communicating the decentral information to the central unit. However, a central management system does not rely on information revelation by better informed decentral units and makes all decisions itself. Consequently, this kind of coordination mechanism will be neglected in my analysis.

I also do not consider transfer prices as a coordination mechanism. Since I assume that there is only one division in the company, there is no exchange of goods between divisions. Hence, a transfer price could only occur for the exchange of goods between headquarters and the division. In fact, some authors have taken the view that the provision of capital by headquarters can be seen as part of an exchange of goods between headquarters and the division. The required interest payments for the provision of capital can be seen as a transfer price.[30] I do not follow this view, since in most of the literature, the expression transfer price usually does not relate to the provision of capital and the corresponding interest payments. Rather it refers to the valuation of an intra-company exchange, mainly between divisions that have the form of a profit center.[31] Therefore, transfer prices as a coordination mechanism can also be neglected in my analysis.

---

[30] See, e.g., Hofmann (2001), p. 162.
[31] See Eccles & White (1988), p. S19.

Hence, I restrict attention to the two coordination mechanisms budgeting and performance measurement systems. Since I explicitly consider a two-person decision context with asymmetric information, incentive problems are of importance. As stand-alone systems, both coordination mechanisms do not address incentive problems explicitly. They have to be linked to incentive systems in order to have an impact on the behavior of divisional managers. There are several ways to link the two coordination mechanisms to incentive mechanisms, depending on the type of incentive problem that is of importance. The following subsection analyzes two combinations of them, namely the use of capital rationing as an incentive device within the capital budgeting procedure and the use of performance-based compensation as an incentive device for performance measurement systems.

2.2.2 Capital Budgeting and Capital Rationing

Relationship Between Capital Budgeting and Capital Rationing

The technique of capital budgeting is referred to as the process of allocating corporate funds to investment projects according to ascertained investment decision rules.[32] Capital rationing is a specific behavior in the capital budgeting process that implies a restriction on investment activity in the form of a fixed budget, such that some profitable projects are rejected. The literature frequently distinguishes between internal and external capital rationing. While internal capital rationing refers to a voluntary restriction on investment activity[33], external capital rationing is due to constraints imposed by the external capital market.[34] I do not consider external capital rationing in this work, since I focus on intra-company incentive issues. In contrast, I analyze internal capital rationing as an incentive device for divisional managers.

For budgeting procedures, the problem of truthful reporting of information to central management is an important issue.[35] This is par-

[32] See, e.g., Copeland & Weston (1988), p. 26.

[33] See, e.g., Zhang (1997).

[34] See, e.g., Lorie & Savage (1955); Weingartner (1977); Brealey & Myers (1996), pp. 101-105. For a survey on external capital rationing see Matson (1999).

[35] One of the basic result in information economics is the revelation principle, which states that any implementable allocation between a principal and an agent can also be implemented by using a direct revelation mechanism that induces the agent to tell the truth. For the revelation principle, see in particular Myerson (1979). For additional incentive problems within budgeting procedures see Hofmann (2001), pp. 54-55.

ticularly true for capital budgeting, where decisions on budgets highly depend on all available information on investment projects. Central management needs truthful reports from divisional managers in order to make correct decisions with respect to the capital budgeting procedure. Divisional managers are often interested in overstating the true investment cost, because they can use excessive parts of the budget for personal consumption purposes.[36] To elicit truthful reports about for example investment cost from divisional managers, several mechanisms have been developed in the literature for different settings.[37] While theoretically appealing mechanisms like profit sharing or the Groves-mechanism, which base the rewards of divisional managers on other manager's reports about their financial needs, are hardly used in practice and have been heavily criticized in the literature[38], the use of capital rationing is prevalent in corporate budgeting practices.[39] Capital rationing is used as a coordination as well as an incentive device. The following section analyzes capital rationing as an incentive instrument within capital budgeting practices.

A Model of Capital Rationing

Various authors have analyzed the capital budgeting process within firms in a context of (at least) two participants and asymmetric information.[40] To show the basic principles of incentive effects of capital rationing, a formal model is used that is a variant of a model developed by *Antle* and *Eppen*[41].

The model consists of a risk neutral headquarters that acts in the interest of the company's owners and a risk neutral divisional manager.

36 See, e.g., Jensen & Meckling (1976). An alternative but related view is that the manager has a preference for controlling a larger budget, which is sometimes referred to as the desire for empire building, see Arya, et al. (1999); Baldenius (2002); Harris & Raviv (1996).

37 For mechanisms for independent divisions, see, e.g., Weitzman (1976); Osband & Reichelstein (1985); Kirby, et al. (1991); Reichelstein (1992); Trauzettel (1999), pp. 193-217. The Groves-mechanism (see Groves (1973) and Groves & Loeb (1979)) can be applied for multi-divisional firms with dependencies between divisions.

38 See Ewert & Wagenhofer (2003), pp. 574-576.

39 See Gitman & Forrester Jr. (1977); Ferreira & Brooks (1988); Fremgen (1973).

40 See Antle & Eppen (1985); Antle & Fellingham (1990); Antle & Fellingham (1995); Antle, et al. (1999); Harris, et al. (1982); Harris & Raviv (1996); Harris & Raviv (1998); Sappington (1983). For a selective review see Antle & Fellingham (1997).

41 See Antle & Eppen (1985).

Headquarters has to decide on the amount of money to be allocated on a specific investment project within the capital allocation procedure. While both of them know the expected value of the cash inflows from the project, V, the manager has private information about the initial investment cost I. At the time, the investment decision has to be made, she knows I with certainty, while headquarters only knows that I is drawn from an arbitrary probability distribution with positive support on the interval $[\underline{I}, \overline{I}]$ with $F(I)$ and $f(I)$ denoting the cumulative distribution function and density function, respectively.[42]

Headquarters' objective is to maximize the expected net present value of the investment. The manager is interested in maximizing her utility, which is given by the amount of organizational slack S, i.e. the difference between the allocated amount of capital B and the capital I that is needed to undertake the investment. This utility function can be motivated in at least three ways: First, in reality there may be uncertainty over investment cost even for the manager. Although not modelled, uncertainty obviously increases the demand for money in order to be able to invest also in bad states of nature. Second, the manager can spend parts of the capital budget for related but not essential expenditures like, e.g. expensive office equipment, luxurious travelling, etc. Third, the investment cost is not fixed, but can be reduced by the provision of managerial costly effort. Organizational slack reduces the incentive to provide such kind of cost-reducing effort. This feature is not incorporated in the model, but it can be easily shown, that the main results of the model carry over to the case, when the ability to provide cost-reducing effort is included in the model.

In summary, headquarters' problem is to maximize the following objective function

$$\max_{\{S(\cdot),d(\cdot)\}} \int_{\underline{I}}^{\overline{I}} \{-S(I) + d(I)\,(V - I)\}\, f(I)\, dI \qquad (2.1)$$

where $d(\cdot) \in \{0, 1\}$ is a binary function that indicates whether investment is undertaken ($d(\cdot) = 1$) or not ($d(\cdot) = 0$). In this program, headquarters has to consider two sets of constraints. The first set of constraints ensures participation of each manager regardless of the true value of investment cost she faces (participation constraints). To guarantee participation, the manager's utility given by the amount of organi-

42 The main differences to the model of Antle and Eppen are that they have assumed (i) asymmetric information over the rate of return instead of investment cost, and (ii) a probability distribution over a discrete set of states of the world instead of a continuous distribution.

zational slack must be at least her reservation utility, which is assumed to be 0 in my model for all realizations of I.

$$S(I) \geq 0 \; \forall I \tag{2.2}$$

The second set of constraints ensures that it is in the manager's interest to reveal the truth about the investment cost. These constraints are a consequence of the revelation principle[43], which ensures that among the set of possible contracts, the analysis can be restricted to contracts that ask the manager to reveal the true investment cost. The revelation principle requires the principal to commit himself not to renegotiate the terms of the offered contract, after the investment cost is revealed by the agent. This assumption can be justified for example by (not modelled) reputation effects in a repeated relationship. If the manager reports I, when the true investment outlay is I, her utility should be equal to or higher than her utility, if she reports a different $\hat{I}$. Denoting the managers slack $S(I, \hat{I})$ and similarly the investment decision $d(I, \hat{I})$, if the manager reports $\hat{I}$ when the true investment cost is I, the incentive constraints that ensure truth-telling can be written in the following form:

$$S(I, I) \geq S(I, \hat{I}) + d(I, \hat{I})(\hat{I} - I) \; \forall I, \hat{I} \tag{2.3}$$

The solution of this model is standard in the adverse selection literature[44] and proceeds by further analyzing the incentive constraints and substituting the resulting expressions for the slack functions into headquarters' objective. Doing that, headquarters' optimization problem reduces to finding a cut-off level I^*, up to which investment occurs and above which no investment takes place, as given in the following expression:

$$\max_{I} F(I)\,(V - I) \tag{2.4}$$

The first order condition of an interior solution to this optimization problem is given by

$$I^* = V - \frac{F(I^*)}{f(I^*)} \tag{2.5}$$

An immediate implication of this result is that capital rationing occurs. The cut-off level, up to which investment occurs is reduced by

[43] See Myerson (1979); Harris & Townsend (1981).

[44] See, e.g., Fudenberg & Tirole (1992), pp 243-318; Laffont & Tirole (1993).

the term $\frac{F(I^*)}{f(I^*)}$ compared to the first-best case, where the cut-off level is given by $I^{FB} = V$.

To illustrate this result, consider the following numerical example. The expected net present value of the project's cash flows is $V = 1$, and headquarters' believes about the initial investment outlays are uniformly distributed according to $I \sim U[0.5; 1.5]$. The density function of this distribution is

$$f(I) = \begin{cases} 1 & \text{if} \quad 0.5 \leq I \leq 1.5 \\ 0 & \text{otherwise} \end{cases} \tag{2.6}$$

while the cumulative distribution function is

$$F(I) = \begin{cases} 0 & \text{if} \quad I < 0.5 \\ I - 0.5 & \text{if} \quad 0.5 \leq I \leq 1.5 \\ 1 & \text{if} \quad I > 1.5 \end{cases} \tag{2.7}$$

If headquarters knew the true value of I, investment takes place if $I \leq 1$. Since headquarters does not know the true value of I, the optimal cut-off level is determined by the first order condition (2.5), which yields $I^* = 1 - (I^* - 0.5)$. Solving for the optimal cut-off level yields $I^* = 0.75$, which is significantly below the first-best level of $I^{FB} = 1$. If the initial investment outlays are between 0,75 and 1, capital rationing occurs. In this case, headquarters decides not to invest, although the net present value of investment is positive. Figure 2.1 illustrates this result by indicating three areas: the expected net present value received by headquarters, the expected slack received by the manager, and the forgone net present value, which is a consequence of capital rationing. The total of these three areas is the expected net present value of headquarters, if information is symmetrically distributed.

In this model, the occurrence of capital rationing is a consequence of the managerial private information about investment cost. Due to this informational asymmetry, headquarters must compensate the divisional manager by paying an informational rent. If the true investment cost are below 0.75, the manager receives the difference between the actual cost and the cut-off level as organizational slack. Headquarters has to balance the trade-off between reducing the informational rent and increasing the value of the investment project by investing in as many states as possible, where investment has a positive net present value. The capital budgeting mechanism, analyzed in this section is in fact a central mechanism. The manager has private information, but since she reports her information truthfully, headquarters can decide centrally on investment. Due to the revelation principle, this result of central decision-making is indeed optimal and cannot be improved by a delegated mechanism. However, it may be possible to replicate the central mechanism by a delegation mechanism, which delegates the investment decision to the manager, and which yields the same result as the optimal revelation mechanism.[45] Therefore, a similar capital budgeting procedure as analyzed above may also apply in settings where investment decisions are made decentrally.

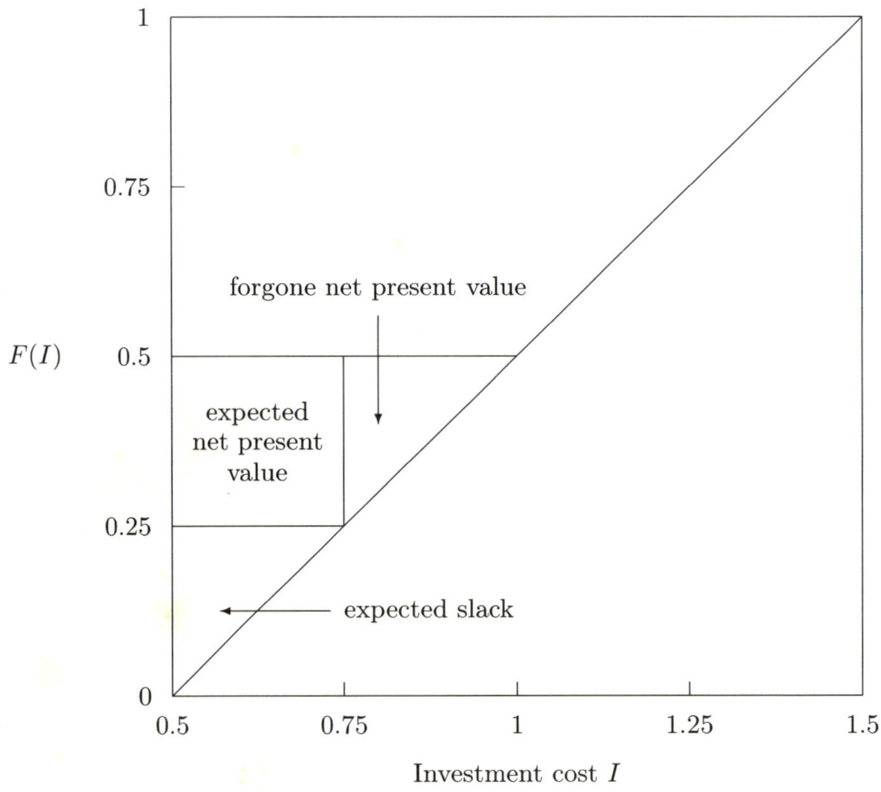

Fig. 2.1. Expected net present value and expected slack

[45] See also Laffont & Tirole (1986).

Empirical Results on Capital Rationing

The use of capital rationing is prevalent in corporate capital budgeting practice. Capital rationing occurs in two different forms: Either, headquarters uses a hurdle rate that is above a company's cost of capital, or it limits the financial resources to be allocated to the divisions such that profitable projects have to be rejected. In both cases, headquarters will forgo some projects with positive net present value, which cannot be explained in a neoclassical framework. Empirical evidence has been given for both practices.

Poterba and *Summers* asked the CEOs at Fortune 1000 firms about the firms's hurdle rates. They found that the "average discount rate applied to constant-dollar cash flows was 12.2%, distinctly higher than equity holders' average rates of return and much higher than the return on debt during the past half century".[46] Similarly, *Ross* studied the capital budgeting practice of twelve large manufacturers. He found that hurdle rates for investment projects were at about 15% with some companies having hurdle rates up to 60%.[47] Hence, companies seem to use hurdle rates significantly above the cost of capital.

Empirical evidence can also be found on the limitation of financial resources within firms. *Gitman* and *Forrester* found that more than half of the respondents to a survey of major U.S. firms indicated that their firm made a competitive allocation of a fixed budget to competing projects[48], which suggests that at least some projects with positive net present value do not receive the necessary budgets. *Ferreira* and *Brooks* as well as *Fremgen* reported even higher incidents of rationing, namely 60,3% and 73%, respectively.[49] Hence capital rationing is a prevalent phenomenon and the implications of uncertainty and managerial flexibility to theoretical predictions on capital rationing promise to yield further insights into capital rationing practice.

2.2.3 The Use of Performance-Based Compensation

Performance Measurement Systems and Performance-Based Compensation

Performance measurement systems in the context of investment decisions usually assume a higher degree of delegation than capital budgeting procedures. These coordination systems define objectives for the

[46] Poterba & Summers (1995), p. 43.

[47] See Ross (1986).

[48] See Gitman & Forrester Jr. (1977).

[49] See Ferreira & Brooks (1988) and Fremgen (1973).

divisional managers that are measurable and are associated with the overall objectives of the company. Maximizing the value of a firm, and more precisely, maximizing the net present value of their assets and projects is a common objective for companies as well as divisions within a firm.[50] However, the net present value must include not only the value of the projects in place, but also the value of opportunities that are a consequence of the existing assets and projects[51], which is often referred to as the value of the real options of a company.[52] This value reflects the value of all future cash in- and outflows, given the best managerial strategy that optimally reacts to realizations of uncertain states of the world.

The main drawback of the net present value (including the real option value) as a performance measure is its lacking observability.[53] For listed firms, the value of all shares could serve as an approximative value for the net present value at the company's level. However at the divisional level, this approximation is generally not available. If observability is required for a performance measure, forecasts like for example cash flow forecasts have to be excluded from the set of possible performance measures, since these values cannot be observed.[54] In this case this set includes for instance realized cash flows and realized accounting numbers.[55]

To provide proper incentives for divisional managers with respect to their investment decisions, the performance measurement system and the performance measures have to be linked to an incentive system. An important part of an incentive system is performance-based compensation, which links compensation to the value of certain performance measures. The design of the optimal compensation contract for divisional managers can be broken into the following stages:[56]

- choosing the right performance measure or the right set of performance measures,

---

[50] For a justification of this objective, see, e.g., Brealey & Myers (1996), pp. 17-27; Schmidt (1990), pp. 27-28.

[51] See in particular the early contribution by Hart (1940).

[52] For comprehensive treatments of this topic see Dixit & Pindyck (1994); Trigeorgis (1996); Copeland & Antikarov (2001); Hommel, et al. (2003).

[53] General requirements for performance measures are depicted for instance in Hax (1989), pp. 163-168; Laux (1995), p. 156; Küpper (1998), pp. 527-528; Küpper (2001), pp. 227-229. Observability is discussed in detail by Riegler (2000), p. 37.

[54] See Küpper (2001), p. 228.

[55] For a discussion of their relative advantages see Reichelstein (2000); Wagenhofer & Riegler (1999).

[56] For a similar differentiation see Banker & Datar (1989), p. 22.

- designing the performance measure,
- designing the compensation contract based on this measure.

In this work, I focus on the second issue, which is a question of high practical relevance, since there are a lot of recommendations by theorists as well as practitioners on how to design in particular accounting-based measures of performance. However, the first and the third issue will also be shortly reviewed.

Choosing the Performance Measure

A quite general result on the question, which measure should be chosen to evaluate the actions of a divisional manager is *Holmström's* informativeness result.[57]. It states that each performance measure that is informative about the agent's act should be considered for contracting purposes.[58] With respect to investment decisions, all cash flows associated with the investment project are informative about the agent's action choice. Hence, cash flows should be the basic figures for performance evaluation purposes. However, one of the particularities of investment decisions is their property that the positive consequences of these decisions only realize in the long run.

There are at least two problems of using realized cash flows for managerial performance evaluation. If managers have shorter time horizons than headquarters or the owners of a company, managers prefer investment projects, where the benefits realize faster than projects where the benefits realize more slowly. These different time preferences can lead to incentive problems in selecting the right projects. With cash flows as a performance measure, the divisional manager not necessarily undertakes all projects with positive net present value and only those. A second problem related to the use of realized cash flows as a performance measure is the fact that realized cash flows generally reflect only a very small part of the information that is available for contracting purposes. They do not contain information on the interest rate that has been used for calculating the cost of capital, although this information is usually available for headquarters. Moreover, often the life-time of an investment project can be estimated with reasonable reliability. This information is also not reflected in realized cash flows.

Performance measures, which contain such kind of information, are periodic income measures like for instance accounting income and resid-

[57] See Holmström (1979), pp. 83-84.

[58] For a detailed description of the informativeness principle see Budde (2000), pp. 44 et seqq.

ual income.[59] Accounting income differs from cash flows by some accruals. The most important accrual for investment decisions is the capitalization of the initial investment cash outlay and the subsequent depreciation. Restricting myself to this accrual, accounting income Inc_t in period t then takes the following form, assuming that the investment project is undertaken in $t = 0$ and generates cash flows in T subsequent periods:

$$Inc_t = CF_t - d_t \cdot b, \tag{2.8}$$

where CF_t denotes the cash flow in period t, b denotes the initial cash investment, and d_t denotes the fraction of the initial cash investment that is depreciated in t. The depreciation schedule usually has the property that $\sum_{t=1}^{T} d_t = 1$, meaning that the total sum of depreciation equals the initial investment outlay.[60] Obviously, accounting income uses more information than cash flows, because the depreciation schedule contains information about the lifetime of the investment project. However, information on the interest rate or the cost of capital is not part of the accounting income measure.

This information is used in a different class of performance measures, which are based on residual income, defined as the difference between accounting income and interest charges on the value of the invested capital:

$$RI_t = Inc_t - r \cdot V_{t-1} = CF_t - d_t \cdot b - r \cdot V_{t-1}, \tag{2.9}$$

where residual income in period t is denoted by RI_t, r is the interest rate that is used for calculating the interest charges and V_{t-1} is the (book) value of the assets in place in period $t-1$. The latter depends on the depreciation method, such that $V_t = V_{t-1} - d_t \cdot b$, and $V_0 = b$.

Realized residual income uses information on the length of the investment project as well as on the cost of the invested capital. Besides that, it has the appealing property that under certain conditions the sum of all discounted future residual incomes is equal to the net

[59] There are a lot more than these three types of performance measures, like for instance return on investment (RoI), or cash value added (CVA). I restrict attention to the choice between these three measures, because the recent theoretical debate has largely focused on these measures, see, e.g., Pfeiffer (2003); Reichelstein (2000); Wagenhofer (2003). For an overview, see Hachmeister (2002), pp. 1388-1393; Hebertinger (2001), pp. 65-194.

[60] This assumption is consistent with the clean surplus relation, see, Ohlson (1995); Feltham & Ohlson (1995).

present value of a project.[61] This important equivalence result does not hold for accounting income, where no interest charges are considered. Hence, it is not surprising that theorists as well as practitioners propose the use of residual income for performance evaluation purposes.[62] In simplified formal settings of delegated investment decision-making, Rogerson (1997), Reichelstein (1997), and subsequently various other authors showed that within their models residual income turns out to be the only optimal performance measure among a wide spectrum of alternative performance measures. For this reason I restrict attention to residual income as a performance measure. The objective of chapter 4 und 5 is to analyze different design alternatives for this measure in the case of investments under uncertainty with embedded flexibility.

Design of the Performance Measure

Restricting myself to residual income as a performance measure, an important question is how to design important aspects of this measure. The defining equation (2.9) can be used as a starting point to highlight various design alternatives. These include the choice of different depreciation schedules, alternative capitalization rules for assets, the choice of the interest rate, and the asset base that is used to calculate the capital charges in the residual income measure.

The choice among different depreciation schedules for the residual income measure is an issue of ongoing research. In practice, the use of straight-line depreciation is dominant.[63] However, theory has pointed to serious problems of this schedule for performance evaluation purposes, in particular, if depreciation does not reflect the true economic loss of value of the asset.[64] Instead of that, different alternatives have been proposed. A lot of attention has been devoted to the so called relative benefit depreciation schedule[65], which has been shown to be the only depreciation schedule that induces a manager to invest in projects with

[61] This equivalence result is also known under the term Preinreich-Lücke-Theorem, see Preinreich (1937); Lücke (1955).

[62] A survey on the theoretical literature on residual income can be found in Bromwich & Walker (1998). Practitioners are marketing residual income measures under different labels, the most prominent of which is probably Economic Value Added (see Stewart III (1991); Hostettler (1997); O'Hanlon & Peasnell (1998); Stern, et al. (2001)). A survey of capital budgeting practices of the Fortune 1000 companies indicated that 53,9% are using EVA at least sometimes, see Ryan & Ryan (2002).

[63] For a discussion of possible reasons see Green, et al. (2002).

[64] For a detailed criticism see Solomons (1965), pp. 134 et seqq.

[65] See Reichelstein (1997), p. 168; Baldenius, et al. (1999), p. 59.

positive net present value and only in those projects. Although this result is subject to rather restrictive assumptions on the distribution of information between central management and a divisional manager, it provides theoretical guidance in evaluating alternative depreciation schedules.

The performance evaluation literature does not discuss capitalization rules for investments as profoundly as depreciation schedules. The reason is probably that this literature, as discussed earlier, takes a very simple view on investment decisions. For these simple investments, capitalizing the initial cash investment and subsequently depreciating it seems to be quite reasonable and under certain conditions even optimal.[66]. If investment projects have a more complicated form, because they includes for instance the option to abandon the project, this simple capitalization rule has to be challenged. An example of a different capitalization rule is the treatment of research and development expenditures under US-GAAP. Under these rules, capitalization of research and development expenditures, although clearly investment expenditures, is prohibited.[67] The practitioner oriented literature partly makes some recommendations how to adjust the external accounting treatment of research and development expenditures for performance evaluation purposes including a different capitalization rule.[68] However, there are no systematic recommendations, how to capitalize the expenditures for investment projects with inherent uncertainty and flexibility, and how to treat the option value.

A third design alternative is the choice of the interest rate and the asset base for the calculation of the capital charge in the residual income measure. Interestingly, most of the literature assumes the use of book values as opposed to market values[69] for the asset base. This is in sharp contrast to some recommendations in the regulation literature, where the calculation of the cost of capital sometimes relies on market values.[70] Two possible arguments for the use of book values for perfor-

[66] See Reichelstein (1997).

[67] SFAS 2, which rules the accounting treatment for research and development costs under US-GAAP, requires that R&D generally be expensed as incurred and that each yearŠs total R&D be disclosed in the financial statements.

[68] Stern et al. (2001), p. 21 propose to include R&D expenses in the balance sheet and amortize it "over the period of years during which these research outlays are expected to have an impact."

[69] See, e.g., Christensen, et al. (2002), p. 6; Egginton (1995), p. 203; Rogerson (1997), p. 785; Velthuis (2003), p. 121.

[70] Busse von Colbe (2002), p. 6 and Küpper (2002), p. 52-53 propose the use of market values as asset base for regulated industries. For a critical discussion see Pedell (2003), p. 6-22.

mance evaluation purposes are that for corporate investments, market values in many cases simply do not exist, or they are subject to huge fluctuations that are beyond the manager's control. While I do not question the use of book values in this work, I add some arguments to the use of specific interest rates to the debate in chapter 5. In this debate, there are quite different recommendations on the table. Textbooks and practitioners often recommend the use of the cost of acquiring investment capital, for which the weighted-average cost of capital (WACC) is commonly used.[71] The concept of Economic Value Added (EVA), an approach based on residual income, also makes use of the WACC for calculating the capital charge.[72] *Christensen, Feltham,* and *Wu* point out that there are some flaws in this recommendation.[73] First, within the assumptions and the specific setting of their model, they find that it is wrong to adjust the capital charge for market risk, as is done in the WACC. Second, firm-specific risk, which is not part of the WACC, since investors can avoid it through diversification, has an impact on the manager. The required adjustment of the capital charge rate depends on the question if the manager has private pre-decision information or not.[74] Chapter 5 of this work addresses the problem of determining capital charges for investments that include real options.

Design of the Compensation Function

The compensation function, which ties the value of the performance measure to the compensation of the manager can be characterized along several lines. A prevalent and in the theoretical literature frequently used form is the linear compensation function. An increase of the performance measure linearly increases the value of the compensation, and there is no upper or lower bound on compensation. Two alternative forms are convex and concave functions. Stock options are an example for a convex compensation structure, since there is a lower, but no upper bound on compensation. Compensation agreements with an upper bound are an example for concave compensation functions. Sometimes the compensation function is concave in some regions and convex in other regions. An example frequently used in practical compensation

[71] See, e.g., Anthony & Govindarajan (2000), p. 256; Hilton, et al. (2000), p. 839; Horngren, et al. (1999), p. 663-664. For an early discussion see Rudolph (1986), pp. 892-898.

[72] See, Stern et al. (2001); pp. 19-20; Horngren et al. (1999), pp. 664-666.

[73] See Christensen et al. (2002).

[74] A criticism of using the WACC can also be found in Velthuis (2003), pp. 123-128.

agreements is a function that is linear for some values of the performance measure, but has an upper and lower bound for very low and very high values of the performance measure.

I restrict myself in this work to the use of linear compensation functions. There are two reasons for this restriction. First, much of the incentive literature also takes this view, i.e. it exogenously assumes that contracts are linear functions of the performance measure.[75] Second, among the relatively simple forms of compensation functions, as described above, one can expect less distortions of investment incentives from the linear form compared to concave or convex functions.[76]

A second important property of compensation functions is the intensity, with which they provide incentives. The intensity of incentives is in particular relevant for operational or effort incentives, since in this case problems of risk-sharing and managerial effort aversion are important. In a standard moral hazard setting with the assumption of linear contracts[77], the intensity of incentives depends on four factors:[78]

- the incremental profits created by additional effort,
- the precision with which the desired activities are assessed,
- the agent's risk tolerance, and
- the agent's responsiveness to incentives.

Although the intensity undoubtedly also affects investment incentives, I do not focus on the intensity of incentives in this work, because the intensity is regarded as an additional parameter of a compensation system that mainly addresses operational incentive issues. For investment incentive issues, the structure and design of the performance measure is considered to be of more importance.

2.2.4 Comparison of Capital Rationing and Performance-Based Compensation

Despite some similarities, capital rationing and performance-based compensation exhibit a lot of differences with respect to the situations they can be applied and the incentive effects which they aim at. Table 2.3 summarizes differences and similarities of both instruments.

---

[75] See, e.g., Bushman & Indjejikian (1993); Bushman, et al. (2000); Christensen et al. (2002); Feltham & Xie (1994); Reichelstein (1997); Dutta & Reichelstein (2002b).

[76] See, e.g., Jensen (2001).

[77] See section 2.3.2.

[78] See Milgrom & Roberts (1992), p. 221.

Table 2.3. Comparison of capital rationing and performance-based compensation as incentive devices

	Capital Rationing	Performance-based Compensation
Types of addressed incentive problems	investment incentives	investment and operational incentives
Input- or output-orientation	only input	input and output
Extent of delegation	no delegation	complete delegation
Communication necessary	yes	no
Source of managerial utility	slack resources	compensation payments
Distribution of information	asymmetrically	asymmetrically

While capital rationing exclusively addresses investment incentive problems, performance-based compensation can be used for a broader scope of applications. The latter helps to provide incentives for investment decisions as well as operational effort decisions. One of the reasons is that the latter tries to influence input and output, whereas capital rationing rather affects the input side and here mainly the initial investment outlay.

Capital rationing has to be distinguished from performance-based compensation with respect to the degree of delegation.[79] Capital rationing is a relatively centralized procedure that makes use of the divisional manager's information by trying to induce a truthful report. Based on this report, the investment decision can be made centrally. Performance-based compensation does not try to elicit a truthful report, but completely delegates the investment decision to the divisional manager. Since capital rationing requires a high quality of information at headquarters, the divisional managers either have to communicate truthfully all available information to headquarters, or headquarters has to have a good understanding about divisional operations. On the other hand, performance-based compensation does not require communication, since the compensation payments are designed such that the interests of headquarters and the divisional managers become aligned. The compensation payments serve as the major source of utility for the divisional manager. If she does not get any performance-based com-

[79] See also Taggart Jr. (1987) and Kester & Taggart Jr. (1989).

pensation, as is the case in capital rationing, the divisional manager's utility may arise from the allocation of slack resources.[80]

Besides these differences, there is at least one aspect, capital rationing and performance-based compensation have in common. Both are instruments that have been developed because of the existence of asymmetrically distributed information in decentralized organizations with divisional manager being better informed about decision-relevant facts than headquarters. This is the reason why this analysis focuses on both instruments and their effects in settings where investment decisions have some real options features.

2.3 Appropriateness of Various Theoretical Methodologies for the Analysis

2.3.1 Requirements for the Employed Methodology

The objective of this work is a theoretical analysis of incentive problems for investment decision making, when new information arrives after the initial decision has been made. From these types of problems under consideration, some requirements for the employed theoretical methodology can be derived.

First and most importantly, the methodology must be able to address a two (or more) person decision context with asymmetric information. Additionally, the methodology must be able to deal with different objective functions for the involved parties, since divisional managers and headquarters usually have different goals.

Second, the methodology must be able to deal with dynamic problems, since I am interested in situations, where the arrival of new information may lead to a change of actions. While a theoretical analysis of investment incentive problems has been widely accomplished in static models,[81] the arrival of new information and a possible change in the course of actions makes a dynamic modelling mandatory.

Two methodologies have been mainly used in the literature to address investment incentive issues, namely principal-agent models and the goal congruence models. The following subsections describe and compare these methodologies with respect to their appropriateness for the present analysis.

---

[80] See Baldenius (2002) for a model, which combines performance-based compensation with private benefits of controlling larger projects. The latter is quite similar to a desire for slack.

[81] See, e.g., Antle & Eppen (1985); Harris & Raviv (1996); Harris & Raviv (1998); Bernardo et al. (2001).

2.3.2 Principal-Agent Models

Principal-agent models deal with the problem, how to design an optimal contract between two or more parties, when there is asymmetric information between them, and everybody's input is necessary to obtain an output.[82] They are part of the broader theory of incentives[83] or contract theory[84]. A standard classification of principal-agent models distinguishes between moral hazard and adverse selection models.[85] Moral hazard models deal with the problem, when both principal and agent are symmetrically informed at the time of contracting. After contracting, the agent chooses an unobservable action, which affects the observable and usually contractible output. Adverse selection models address issues of pre-contractual private information. Usually, the agent is better informed than the principal before entering the contract.[86] The objective of the principal is to maximize his surplus by limiting the informational rent, which he has to pay to the agent for her private information. The expression contract has to be defined broadly in this context. A capital budgeting procedure, for instance, can be viewed as such a contract. Although the agent is already employed, the results of a capital budgeting procedure have an additional impact on the utility of the manager. Here, it is reasonable to assume that a manager has such kind of pre-contractual private information.

The incentive literature has analyzed investment incentive issues more frequently with adverse selection models than with moral hazard models.[87] The latter rather have been applied to analyze operational incentive issues due to their focus on incentives for the provision of managerial effort. From a modelling perspective, it is difficult to address incentive issues with moral hazard models. A general moral hazard model[88] can be solved only under very specific conditions.[89] Therefore,

[82] For an overview over applications of principal-agent models in different areas of business research see Jost (2001b).

[83] See Laffont & Martimort (2002).

[84] See Hart & Holmström (1987); Brousseau & Glachant (2002).

[85] See Arrow (1985), p. 38; Jost (2001a), pp. 23-31.

[86] Of course, the opposite information structure is also possible, i.e. the principal is better informed than the agent at the time of contracting.

[87] Antle & Fellingham (1997), p. 905, argue that "given the variety of institutions available for risk sharing (banks, insurance companies, casinos), the possibility exists that it may not be economically insightful to resolve the risk sharing problem in a capital investment setting."

[88] See Holmström (1979).

[89] See Grossman & Hart (1983); Rogerson (1985); Jewitt (1988). See also Mirrlees (1999).

many authors rely on the so-called LEN-model, which exogenously assumes linear contracts between the principal and the agent, an exponential utility function, and a normally distributed noise term.[90] If an agent can decide whether to undertake an investment with an uncertain outcome or not, the assumption of normally distributed outcomes, which is necessary for applying the LEN-framework, is at least problematic. It is difficult to justify the same noise term for the outcome variable, regardless whether the investment has been undertaken or not. For this reason, I do not use moral hazard models in this work.

Despite this criticism on moral hazard models for the purposes of this work, the use of principal-agent models has some important advantages. First, principal-agent models are generally able to address problems with asymmetric information between two or more parties, like for example headquarters and divisional managers. Second, the optimal contract between these parties is an endogenous result of these models and has not to be specified exogenously. Moreover, contracting costs are part of these considerations. Hence the trade-off between the provision of incentives and reducing the compensation expenditures can be analyzed. Therefore these models are able to yield important insights for the practical design of contracts.

However, the use of principal-agent models also is associated with some disadvantages and has been heavily criticized in the literature.[91] One of the disadvantages is the requirement of exactly specifying the form of the utility functions and the probability distributions. The results often crucially depend on the specific characteristics of these forms and are sometimes not robust against minor changes. However, in practice it is difficult to exactly state the utility function of a divisional manager in order to derive the optimal contract. Practical contracts have to be robust over a range of utility functions and specifications of uncertainty. Currently, this requirement cannot be satisfactorily modelled in principal-agent models. A second disadvantage lies in the growing complexity of principal-agent models, in particular, if dynamic aspects are added to the model.[92] On the one hand, there are technical impediments that prevent the derivation of closed-form solutions. On the other hand, issues of contractual commitment and renegotiation proofness arise, where theory is still developing.[93]

---

[90] See Spremann (1987); Holmström & Milgrom (1987); Wagenhofer & Ewert (1993).

[91] For a detailed general criticism of agency-theory see Meinhövel (1999), pp. 107-170.

[92] See, e.g., Lambert (2001) pp. 77-79.

[93] Recent papers on these issues include Indjejikian & Nanda (1999); Dutta & Reichelstein (2002c); Sliwka (2002); Christensen, et al. (2003).

In summary, the use of principal-agent models can yield some important qualitative insights for dealing with investment incentive issues, but the limitations of this approach have to be carefully analyzed for each case.

2.3.3 Goal Congruence Models

Problems of choosing performance measures for controlling investment decisions have been partly addressed by a certain type of models, which are henceforth referred to as goal congruence models. These kind of models make some simplifying assumptions compared to principal-agent models, since they do not model contractual costs as principal-agent models do. They rather assume that contractual costs are negligible small compared to the results of the investment decisions and therefore do not enter the formal analysis. The criterion of *goal congruence* defines as a desirable property of a performance measure that "the manager should have an incentive to accept all projects with positive net present value, and only those projects."[94] Various authors have worked with this criterion to analyze design alternatives for accounting measures of performance.[95] Since contractual costs are neglected, the focus of these models is not to derive the form of an optimal contract, like for example the steepness of the compensation function. Rather, they help to select and design the performance measure, on which compensation should be based, while exogenously presuming a certain form of the compensation function.[96] These kind of models allow a more detailed analysis of performance measures than the informativeness result[97], which simply states that an (additional) performance measure is useful for incentive purposes, if it delivers (additional) information about the agent's action choice. While the latter helps to choose the right performance measures, it is not so useful in giving recommendations on the right design of performance measures.

Besides their ability to address issues of asymmetric information between the involved parties, goal congruence models have the appealing property of a reduced mathematical complexity. Depending on the type of problem, the utility functions can take more general forms, and assumptions on probability distributions can sometimes be completely omitted. Therefore, these models give quite robust solutions.

---

[94] Reichelstein (1997), p. 157.

[95] See, e.g., Rogerson (1997); Reichelstein (1997); Gillenkirch & Schabel (2001); Dutta & Reichelstein (2002a).

[96] Frequently, the literature specifies the form of the contract as a linear one.

[97] See Holmström (1979), p. 83-84.

However, their major disadvantage is that contractual costs are neglected on the side of the principal. Hence, using these models is only reasonable in situations, where incentive payments are small compared to the value of projects under consideration. A second disadvantage is that the form of the optimal contract is not derived endogenously. Therefore, even infinitely small values of bonus coefficients suffice to provide sufficient investment incentives. A model based on goal congruence has to give additional reasons outside the model to motivate positive values of bonus coefficients.[98]

Consequently, goal congruence models can be used to analyze incentive properties of different performance measures, even in the context of dynamic investment decision making. However, conclusions on bonus coefficients cannot be drawn. Hence the use of either principal-agent models or goal congruence models depends on the research question to be analyzed. This work makes use of both types of models in order to address a broad set of questions.

[98] An example for such a reason is the need for providing operational incentives in addition to investment incentives, which can be addressed by the steepness of the compensation function. See Dutta & Reichelstein (2002b) for a formalization of this argument.

3

Capital Rationing as an Incentive Instrument for Growth Options

3.1 Relevance of Growth Options for R&D-Investments

The purpose of this chapter is to analyze capital rationing as an incentive device for an investment opportunity that has the form of a growth option by using a formal principal-agent model. A growth option is an investment opportunity which is available, if a company makes an initial investment and the uncertain environment evolves favorable. Only this initial investment decision allows the company to make a follow-up investment. Typical examples for growth options are research and development (R&D) investments, particularly in uncertain markets. Investment activities in research provide options to engage in product development, if the research results are promising. In case of bad news on the results or the product market, the follow-up investment will not be made, i.e., the growth option will not be exercised.[1]

While the valuation of investment opportunities as growth options has been addressed by a large stream of literature in the context of real options[2], at least to my knowledge a formal analysis of incentive issues in the presence of growth options has been remaining undone up to now. There might be two reasons for this fact. First, an analysis of incentive issues and growth options requires a dynamic principal-agent setting. Dynamic agency-settings, however, are difficult to analyze because of a lot of tractability problems[3]. General predictions in these types of models can hardly be made. Second, as pointed out above, growth options

[1] From this definition, it is clear that growth options and abandonment options are just two sides of the same medal. The term growth option emphasizes the decision to continue, while the focus of the abandonment option is the decision to quit the project.

[2] For an overview see, e.g., Dixit & Pindyck (1994); Trigeorgis (1996).

[3] See, e.g., Lambert (2001) pp. 77-79.

frequently appear in the context of R&D investments. Compensating R&D employees on the basis of cash flows from the project is difficult, if not impossible. These cash flows often realize far in the future, when employees have been assigned new tasks within the firm, or when they have already left the firm. Hence, performance-based payment-schemes cannot be used as an efficient incentive device.

Although performance-based payments are inappropriate to motivate R&D employees, there might be another incentive scheme which is particularly important for investment opportunities with growth options. Corporate R&D funds are usually allocated on projects by a capital budgeting procedure which specifies the goals of the project. Headquarters normally has limited information regarding the issue to what extent single expenditures are really necessary for successfully completing the whole project. To some extent, the expenditures lie in the discretion of the manager of the R&D division and she can use them for own purposes without any benefits for headquarters. These excessive funds are organizational slack. My hypothesis is that they provide incentives for employees particularly in the area of R&D investments[4]. Furthermore, the possibility to gain some slack in future periods if uncertainty resolves in a good state of nature may also serve as an incentive scheme. Growth options have exactly this kind of investment structure.

I analyze the incentives provided by organizational slack in a two-period principal-agent setting with both parties being risk-neutral. Headquarters hires a manager who is better informed about the costs of a two stage investment. A conflict of interests arises, because the manager has a preference for organizational slack, which is costly to headquarters. I analyze two scenarios. First, in my basic model I assume that the manager has no own resources. In this case, a severe underinvestment problem occurs. The investment thresholds in each period in terms of investment costs are lower than in the case without an incentive problem. Headquarters responds to the managerial private information by rationing the investment budget in both periods. Second, as a modification of my basic model, I assume that the managerial resource restriction is lowered. One can think of this case in terms of a manager, who is responsible for several projects and can shift excessive funds from one project to another. In this case, the option on future slack from growth opportunities can be used as an incentive device. In order to achieve this option, the manager invests from his own resources. In this way the underinvestment problem is significantly relaxed.

---

[4] Antle & Eppen (1985) have analyzed the role of organizational slack for a single one-period investment project based on the same hypothesis.

The assumption of uniformly distributed investment costs allows me to analyze the effect of uncertainty in each of the periods on the investment thresholds. Two effects have to be taken into account. First, the value of the growth option increases as uncertainty increases. Second, the information rent for the manager increases as uncertainty increases. Most interestingly, an increase in second-period uncertainty leads to a higher investment threshold and therefore a higher probability of investment in the first period. This result confirms similar results in real options models for an asymmetric information case.

The remainder of the chapter is organized as follows. The next section contains a brief literature review. The basic model and a modification of this model is described and analyzed in section 3.3. Section 3.4 discusses the impact of uncertainty on the optimal investment decisions under the special assumption of uniformly distributed investment costs. Section 3.5 gives some implications for capital budgeting procedures.

3.2 Theoretical Results on Capital Budgeting and Growth Options

There are two main streams of literature with relevance for this work. One main area deals with asymmetric information and incentives for capital investments within organizations.[5] Antle & Eppen (1985) have analyzed the role of asymmetric information and organizational slack for the investment thresholds of a single one-period investment project. Their model explains the existence of organizational slack, the rationing of resources within organizations, and hurdle rates that are higher than the costs of capital.[6] Their analysis was extended by Antle & Fellingham (1990) by studying a two-period model. They show that the possibility to distribute slack across the two periods can be used to enhance the level of investment compared to the case of a single period. Consequently, in their model rationing is reduced compared to the one period case. Crucial for their result is the scalability of investment. Without this assumption, no higher level of investment would occur. The main difference between their work and mine is that they assume two independent projects. In particular the execution of the second project does not require investment in the first project. I consider the case of

[5] See Antle & Fellingham (1997) for an overview over models with private information and incentives.

[6] The latter of these results can be found in a number of papers dealing with investment incentive problems, including Holmström & Weiss (1985); Harris & Raviv (1996); Bernardo et al. (2001); Dutta & Reichelstein (2002b).

a single project where continuation of the project depends on the initial decision to invest in the first stage. Harris & Raviv (1998) study a situation, where two projects are available. They focus on the question when a capital allocation decision is delegated to the level below it. In an extension of their basic model, they identify conditions, when delegation is optimal in the case of sequential projects. However, they do not analyze this situation in detail.

Another main area of literature deals with the valuation of capital investments, when there is uncertainty and flexibility to react to new information. Such kind of flexibility embedded in investment opportunities is referred to as real options. Typical examples of real options are timing options[7] or growth options[8]. Dixit & Pindyck (1994) and Trigeorgis (1996) provide a comprehensive treatment of this area of research. However, the focus of this stream of literature are valuation problems. Incentive problems are almost completely neglected in this field of research[9].

With few exceptions, almost no attempts have been made to combine these two areas of research. The pioneering work on this combination at least to my knowledge is Antle et al. (2000). They analyze incentive problems when there is a timing option. With certain distribution assumptions, they show that incentive problems can shut down a timing option that is valuable in the absence of such problems.[10] From a purely methodological point of view, my paper is very close to theirs and relies on many of their calculations. However, the economic implications are strikingly different, as they look at a simple single stage investment project that can be postponed while I analyze a richer two-stage investment project including a growth or abandonment option. Arya & Glover (2001) also analyze a timing option in the presence of incentive problems. In their model, an incentive problem makes the option to wait valuable when it would not have been valuable otherwise.

While the timing option is important in areas like, e.g., real estate investment decisions or the extraction of natural resources[11], their importance for R&D investments is lower. In this field, the possibility

---

[7] See McDonald & Siegel (1986); Ingersoll jr. & Ross (1992); Hu & Bernt (1998).

[8] See Myers (1977); Kester (1984); Kester (1993).

[9] One exception is Bjerksund & Stensland (2000). They study a situation, where a principal who is the owner of a natural gas field must get gas through a pipeline that is operated by an agent to the market.

[10] For an application of their model see Antle et al. (2001).

[11] In general, the value of the timing option is high, when the investment opportunity is exclusive to one party. Competition reduces the option value. See Grenadier (1996).

of dividing investments into several stages becomes more important. The flexibility embedded in these kinds of investment opportunities are growth options. Despite its obvious importance, there has been no work so far on combined growth options and incentive issues.

3.3 Analysis of a Model on Incentive Problems for Growth Options

3.3.1 Model Description

The model consists of a manager and headquarters, which are both risk-neutral. Headquarters is assumed to act in the interest of shareholders. While headquarters has unlimited access to capital, the manager has not. However, the latter has private information about the investment costs of a single sequential investment project. This investment project has the form of a growth option, i.e. it requires a sequence of investment outlays. Only investing in the current stage gives the opportunity to invest in the next stage. Subsequent investment decisions depend on the arrival of new information. A payoff is realized in the last stage.

To keep the model tractable, I focus on the simplest setting, which allows to analyze the growth option. Specifically, I consider a two-stage investment project, which requires two investments at two consecutive points in time. Denote the investment cost at time t with I_t, $t \in \{1, 2\}$. After both investments, the payoff V is realized. This payoff is common knowledge.[12] I assume that the manager has some private information about investment costs. At time $t = 1$, he knows I_1 with certainty, while headquarters believes it is drawn from a probability distribution with positive support on the interval $[\underline{I}_1, \overline{I}_1]$. Denote $F(I_1)$ and $f(I_1)$ the cumulative distribution and density functions, respectively. At $t = 1$ both, headquarters and the manager have the same expectations about the subsequent investment cost in $t = 2$. They believe, I_2 is from the interval $[\underline{I}_2, \overline{I}_2]$ with the cumulative distribution function $G(I_2)$ and the density function $g(I_2)$. I_1 and I_2 are assumed to be independently distributed.[13] I further assume that both distributions F and G satisfy a usual regularity condition. The inverse hazard rates, $H_1(I_1) = F(I_1)/f(I_1)$ and $H_2(I_2) = G(I_2)/g(I_2)$ increase in I_1 and I_2 over their respective supports. Many common distributions like the uniform and the normal

[12] Because I have assumed risk-neutrality of both parties, one can think about the final payoff in terms of its expected value.

[13] This assumption is necessary to achieve tractability of the problem. Relaxing this assumption would strongly complicate the analysis.

distribution fulfill this property. After investing in $t = 1$, the manager learns I_2 while headquarters still has the same expectations on it.

To undertake the investment, the manager must get the capital input I_t from headquarters. I assume, that funds are provided by a capital budgeting procedure, which allocates a certain capital budget B_t, $t \in \{1, 2\}$ to the manager in each of the two points in time and specifies, whether the investment should be undertaken or not. To provide a conflict of interest between the manager and headquarters, I assume the manager can consume any capital in excess of the amount spent into the investment project. This amount is called organizational slack. The manager has a preference for organizational slack S_t, which is given by $S_t = B_t - I_t$ in each period.

Both, headquarters and the manager use the same discount factor q to discount future investment costs, slack, or the payoff in the second period.[14] The decisions to invest are represented by two decision functions $d_1(I_1)$ and $d_2(I_1, I_2)$ for the two periods, which map the set of possible realizations of investment costs into the binary set $\{0, 1\}$. If $d_i = 0$, no investment occurs in period i. $d_i = 1$ means, investment takes place. The form of the investment opportunity as a growth option implies that investment in the second period only takes place, if investment in the first period has occurred. Therefore, $d_2(I_1, I_2) = 1$, only if $d_1(I_1) = 1$.

Headquarters can use organizational slack as an instrument to provide incentives for the manager to tell the truth about investment costs in each of the two points in time. Specifically, headquarters designs an optimal mechanism consisting of the decision rules $d_1(\hat{I}_1)$ and $d_2(\hat{I}_1, \hat{I}_2)$ and the transfers of organizational slack $S_1(\hat{I}_1)$ and $S_2(\hat{I}_1, \hat{I}_2)$ in addition to the investment costs depending on the manager's report about investment costs $\hat{I}_1$ and $\hat{I}_2$, respectively. Importantly, the true investment costs I_1 and I_2 are assumed to be unobservable and unverifiable by headquarters. Therefore, contracts cannot be written on I_1 and I_2 directly. The timeline of the model is summarized in figure 3.1.

Headquarters objective function is to maximize the following expression

$$\max_{\{S_1(\cdot), S_2(\cdot,\cdot), d_1(\cdot), d_2(\cdot,\cdot)\}} \int_{\underline{I}_1}^{\overline{I}_1} \int_{\underline{I}_2}^{\overline{I}_2} \{-S_1(I_1) - d_1(I_1)\, I_1 \\ -q[S_2(I_1, I_2) - d_2(I_1, I_2)\,(V - I_2)]\}\, f(I_1)\, g(I_2)\, dI_1\, dI_2 \tag{3.1}$$

[14] Chapter 4 and 5 analyze models, where headquarters and the divisional manager have different discount factors.

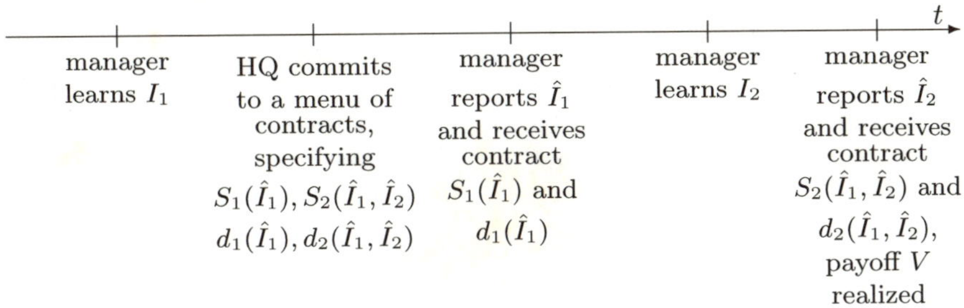

Fig. 3.1. Timeline of the model

subject to three sets of constraints. The first set of constraints ensures that the manager's utility in each period is at least his reservation utility, which is assumed to be 0 in my model. This set of constraints implies limited liability of the manager in each of the two periods. A different interpretation is that the manager can only commit to short-term contracts. If headquarters wants to retain the same manager until the end of the project, it must guarantee his reservation utility in each of both periods.[15]

$$S_1(I_1) + q\,E[S_2(I_1, I_2)] \geq 0 \;\forall I_1 \tag{3.2}$$

$$S_2(I_1, I_2) \geq 0 \;\forall I_1, I_2 \tag{3.3}$$

The second set of constraints ensures truth-telling of the manager. On the one hand, there must be incentives in the second period to tell the truth, given a certain realization of I_1 in the first period. On the other hand, truth-telling in the first period requires taking into account the expected slack in the second period of each first-period cost report.

$$\begin{aligned} S_2(I_1, I_2) \geq\ & S_2(I_1, \hat{I}_2) \\ & + d_2(I_1, \hat{I}_2)(\hat{I}_2 - I_2) \;\forall I_1, I_2, \hat{I}_2 \end{aligned} \tag{3.4}$$

$$\begin{aligned} S_1(I_1) + q\,E[S_2(I_1, I_2)] \geq\ & S_1(\hat{I}_1) + d_1(\hat{I}_1)(\hat{I}_1 - I_1) \\ & + q\,E[S_2(\hat{I}_1, I_2)] \;\forall I_1, \hat{I}_1 \end{aligned} \tag{3.5}$$

with

[15] I change this constraint later in this paper and substitute these participation constraints by a weaker set of constraints, which requires nonnegative utility over both periods and not in each of the two periods.

$$E[S_2(\cdot, I_2)] = \int_{\underline{I}_2}^{\overline{I}_2} S_2(\cdot, I_2)\, g(I_2)\, dI_2 \tag{3.6}$$

The third set of constraints ensures that the investment opportunity has the form of a growth option, i.e. no second-period investment is possible unless there has been investment in the first period.

$$d_1(I_1) \in \{0,1\},\ d_2(I_1, I_2) \in \{0,1\},\ d_2(I_1, I_2) \leq d_1(I_1)\ \forall I_1, I_2 \tag{3.7}$$

3.3.2 Solution of the Model

Now I turn to the solution of the above model. The optimal solution consists of investment thresholds for each period, below which investment takes place and above which not. The optimal investment decisions and the slack functions, which serve as a form of compensation are summarized in the following proposition.

Proposition 3.1. *The following decision functions determine the optimal investment strategy for the optimal pair of investment thresholds* (I_1^*, I_2^*)*:*

$$d_1(I_1) = \begin{cases} 1 & \text{if } I_1 \leq I_1^* \\ 0 & \text{otherwise} \end{cases} \tag{3.8}$$

$$d_2(I_1, I_2) = \begin{cases} 1 & \text{if } I_2 \leq I_2^* \wedge I_1 \leq I_1^* \\ 0 & \text{otherwise} \end{cases} \tag{3.9}$$

Headquarters' problem is solved by the following slack functions:

$$S_1(I_1) = \begin{cases} I_1^* - I_1 & \text{if } I_1 \leq I_1^* \\ q \int_{\underline{I}_2}^{I_2{}^*} (I_2{}^* - I_2)\, g(I_2)\, dI_2 & \text{otherwise} \end{cases} \tag{3.10}$$

$$S_2(I_1, I_2) = \begin{cases} I_2^* - I_2 & \text{if } I_2 \leq I_2^* \wedge I_1 \leq I_1^* \\ 0 & \text{otherwise} \end{cases} \tag{3.11}$$

All proofs of this chapter are in the appendix.

The proposition shows that in each period, headquarters provides a budget, which is equal to the investment threshold, if the reported investment is below the threshold, and which is zero, if it is above. Additionally, headquarters must provide incentives for the manager to tell the truth, if the first period investment cost is above the cut-off level I_1^*. This additional payment reflects the fact that the manager can only receive an expected rent in the second period from the growth option, if he invests in the first period. To prevent the manager from reporting I_1^*, when the true investment cost is higher, headquarters must compensate the manager accordingly. Hence, the pure existence of the growth option in connection with a participation constraint in the second period is costly to headquarters in the sense that it must provide compensation even if no investment takes place. The *ex post*-utility of headquarters might well become negative.

If one thinks about this case in terms of a budgeting procedure, the optimal contract between headquarters and the manager can for instance be written in the following form: In period 1, the manager can choose between accepting the budget $B_1 = I_1^*$ and investing, or accepting the budget $B_1 = q \int_{\underline{I}_2}^{I_2{}^*} (I_2{}^* - I_2)\, g(I_2)\, dI_2$ and not investing. In period 2, the manager can choose between accepting the budget $B_2 = I_2^*$ and investing, or accepting the budget $B_2 = 0$ and not investing. Manager's slack in each period is the difference between the budget and the realized investment cost.

Proposition 3.1 allows me to simplify headquarters' objective function, which is

$$\max_{\{I_1^T, I_2^T\}} \; F(I_1^T)(-I_1^T) + q\, F(I_1^T) G(I_2^T)(V - I_2^T) \qquad (3.12)$$
$$-q\,(1 - F(I_1^T)) \int_{\underline{I}_2}^{I_2{}^T} (I_2{}^T - I_2)\, g(I_2)\, dI_2 .$$

The first term of this objective function is the probability-weighted investment cost in period 1, while the second term is the probability-weighted investment cost and payoff in period 2. The third term reflects the probability-weighted compensation payment, when no investment takes place in the first period. Note that the corner solution $(I_1^T, I_2^T) = (\underline{I}_1, \underline{I}_2)$ results in no investment and a zero value of the objective function. In order to ensure an optimal interior solution, I impose the following restriction on the distribution functions:[16]

$$[F(I_1^*)]^2\, H_1(I_1^*) \geq q\, G(I_2^*)\, H_2(I_2^*) \qquad (3.13)$$

This formulation of headquarters' objective function leads to the following proposition, which characterizes the investment thresholds for investing in each period.

Proposition 3.2. *Suppose (3.13) holds. Then the cut-off levels that determine an optimal interior solution are given by the first order conditions:*

[16] See Appendix for details.

$$I_1^* = q \int_{\underline{I}_2}^{I_2^*} (I_2^* - I_2)\, g(I_2)\, dI_2 - \frac{F(I_1^*)}{f(I_1^*)}, \tag{3.14}$$

$$I_2^* = V - \frac{G(I_2^*)}{g(I_2^*)} \cdot \frac{1}{F(I_1^*)}. \tag{3.15}$$

The interpretation of this result is straightforward. In the second period, headquarters reduces the investment threshold I_2^* by the amount $G(I_2^*)/(g(I_2^*)\, F(I_1^*))$ compared to the simple net present value rule. Headquarters rations investment to some extent in order to reduce the information rents, i.e. slack consumption for the manager. The extent of rationing in the second period is not only determined by the requirement that the manager gets some informational rents in the second period, if investment has taken place in the first period. It also reflects the fact that this informational rents become even more expensive, if the cut-off level in the first period gets near to the lowest possible first period cost. The reason is that in this case, headquarters must also compensate the manager for the second period informational rents in the whole region where $I_1 > I_1^*$ without getting a payoff.

The reduced investment threshold in period 2 has implications for the investment threshold in period 1. Headquarters reduces the discounted expected total surplus of period 2, given the investment threshold in period 2 by the amount $F(I_1^*)/f(I_1^*)$, which reflects the information rent for the manager in the first period.

Since a compensation for the case of no investment is required, headquarters' problem does not always have an optimal interior solution. In particular, consider the case when the initial distribution of I_1 implies a high probability of realizations that are greater than the cut-off level I_1^*. Then headquarters has to compensate the manager with a high probability for bad realizations without getting a payoff. This fact is reflected in condition (3.13), which is sufficient to ensure an optimal interior solution.

3.3.3 Relaxation of the Participation Constraints

I have assumed so far that headquarters' problem is subject to two sets of participation constraints, one for each period. This assumption is consistent with the view that headquarters provides all resources and the manager has no own resources. However, if the manager is responsible for more than one project, she might be able to shift some excess resources from one project to another on her own discretion[17]. In this situation, it might be more reasonable to assume another set of participation constraints, which ensures that the manager's total utility over both periods is nonnegative. The participation constraints in the basic model requiring nonnegative slack in both periods are more demanding, since they do not allow for negative slack in the second period. Hence this assumption significantly relaxes the participation constraint of the manager, because now a negative first-period utility can be compensated by a positive second-period utility. I now analyze the basic model where the two participation constraints (3.2) and (3.3) are substituted by the new participation constraints

$$S_1(I_1) + q\,E[S_2(I_1, I_2)] \geq 0 \;\forall I_1 \tag{3.16}$$

Again, the optimal solution of this model consists of a pair of investment thresholds, one for each period. The optimal investment decisions together with the optimal slack functions are summarized in the following proposition.

Proposition 3.3. *Under constraint (3.16), the following decision functions determine the optimal investment strategy for the optimal pair of investment thresholds* (I_1^{PC}, I_2^{PC})*:*

$$d_1(I_1) = \begin{cases} 1 & \text{if } \; I_1 \leq I_1^{PC} \\ 0 & \text{otherwise} \end{cases} \tag{3.17}$$

$$d_2(I_1, I_2) = \begin{cases} 1 & \text{if } \; I_2 \leq I_2^{PC} \wedge I_1 \leq I_1^{PC} \\ 0 & \text{otherwise} \end{cases} \tag{3.18}$$

Headquarters' problem is solved by the following slack functions:

$$S_1(I_1) = \begin{cases} I_1^{PC} - I_1 \\ -q \int_{\underline{I}_2}^{I_2{}^{PC}} (I_2{}^{PC} - I_2)\, g(I_2)\, dI_2 & \text{if } \; I_1 \leq I_1^{PC} \\ 0 & \text{otherwise} \end{cases} \tag{3.19}$$

$$S_2(I_1, I_2) = \begin{cases} I_2^{PC} - I_2 & \text{if } \; I_2 \leq I_2^{PC} \wedge I_1 \leq I_1^{PC} \\ 0 & \text{otherwise} \end{cases} \tag{3.20}$$

Now, in period two headquarters provides a budget, which is equal to the investment threshold, if the reported investment is below the threshold, and which is zero, if it is above as in the case before. But

[17] See Schiller (2001) for a similar assumption. Laux (2001) shows, how the limited-liability constraint relaxes, if multiple projects are combined under the management of a single manager.

the first period budget is different. It is reduced by the expected slack in period 2 given the investment threshold of the second period. The manager has to provide own resources to fill the difference between the budget and the investment threshold. In this way, the expected second period slack is fully extracted.

Thus, the objective function of headquarters can be rewritten by

$$\max_{\{I_1^T, I_2^T\}} F(I_1^T)\left(-I_1^T + q\int_{\underline{I}_2}^{{I_2}^T} ({I_2}^T - I_2)\, g(I_2)\, dI_2\right) \\ + q\, F(I_1^T) G(I_2^T)(V - I_2^T). \tag{3.21}$$

The first term of this objective function is the cumulative probability of the first period investment cost being lower than or equal to the investment threshold I_1^T times the first period budget. The second term is as in the basic model the probability-weighted investment cost and payoff in period 2. Again, this formulation of headquarters' objective function allows me to derive the first order conditions which result in the following proposition for the investment thresholds for investing in each period.

Proposition 3.4. *Under the relaxed participation constraint (3.16), the optimal interior cut-off levels of the growth option are given by*

$$I_1^{PC} = q\int_{\underline{I}_2}^{I_2^{PC}} (V - I_2)\, g(I_2)\, dI_2 - \frac{F(I_1^{PC})}{f(I_1^{PC})} \tag{3.22}$$

$$I_2^{PC} = V \tag{3.23}$$

In the second period, the manager receives a budget which equals the payoff V. Thus, headquarters' surplus in the second period is 0. But the whole slack of the second period is extracted in the first period. This is the well-known hidden-information case with both parties being risk-neutral and unlimited liability of the agent. Note that the second period utility of the manager might be negative for some realizations of I_2.

3.3.4 Comparison of the Investment Rules

Now I compare the two cases with different participation constraints. The first best solution serves as a benchmark for these two cases. The values of the decision functions in the first best case are as above

$$d_1(I_1) = \begin{cases} 1 & \text{if} \quad I_1 \leq I_1^{FB} \\ 0 & \text{otherwise} \end{cases} \tag{3.24}$$

$$d_2(I_1, I_2) = \begin{cases} 1 & \text{if} \quad I_2 \leq I_2^{FB} \wedge I_1 \leq I_1^{FB} \\ 0 & \text{otherwise} \end{cases} \tag{3.25}$$

It can easily be shown that the optimal investment thresholds in the first best case are

$$I_1^{FB} = q \int_{\underline{I}_2}^{V} (V - I_2)\, g(I_2)\, dI_2, \tag{3.26}$$

$$I_2^{FB} = V. \tag{3.27}$$

The investment threshold in the second period equals the payoff of the investment. In the first period, the investment threshold is the discounted expected surplus of the second period. Therefore, the total value of the investment opportunity X^{FB} including the growth option is *ex ante*

$$X^{FB} = \int_{\underline{I}_1}^{I_1^{FB}} (-I_1)\, f(I_1)\, dI_1 + q \int_{\underline{I}_2}^{I_2^{FB}} (V - I_2)\, g(I_2)\, dI_2 \tag{3.28}$$

Note that the arrival of new information between the first and the second period results in an option value. The second-stage investment will only be made, if this information is favorable. Without this flexibility, the investment criterion would simply be 'invest, if the expected present value of the payoff is at least as high as the expected present value of the two investment costs'.

Now I compare the investment thresholds in the different cases. The following unequation describes the relation between the investment thresholds in the second period:

$$I_2^* \leq I_2^{PC} = I_2^{FB} = V. \tag{3.29}$$

The investment threshold in the case, when a single participation constraint over both periods applies, equals the first best investment threshold, while the investment threshold in the case, when the participation constraints requires nonnegative utility for the manager in each period is weakly lower.

In the first period, the following expression describes the relationship between the investment thresholds:

$$I_1^* \leq I_1^{PC} \leq I_1^{FB}. \tag{3.30}$$

In period one, even the investment threshold of the single participation constraint is weakly lower than in the first best case. The reason is that headquarters wants to limit the information rents of the manager and therefore reduces the investment threshold. In the basic model, the investment threshold is lowest. Headquarters' discounted expected surplus in the second period is lower than in the case when a single participation constraint over both periods applies. Therefore, the investment threshold is reduced.

This result can also be interpreted in terms of investment hurdle rates. Hurdle rates will be highest, when the participation constraints require nonnegative utility of the manager in each of the two periods and will be lowest in the first best case.

3.4 Changing Uncertainty over Investment Costs

In order to analyze the effects of different degrees of uncertainty over investment costs on the optimal investment thresholds at t_1 and t_2, I turn to a special case. That case allows a better understanding of uncertainty on investment behavior in the presence of a growth option and an incentive problem. I assume that investment costs at t_1 and t_2 are uniformly distributed according to $I_1 \sim U[\alpha V - \sigma_1, \alpha V + \sigma_1]$ and $I_2 \sim U[V - \sigma_2, V + \sigma_2]$, with $0 < \sigma_1 \leq \alpha V$, $0 < \sigma_2 \leq V$, and $\alpha > 0$. This formulation means that I_2 is symmetrically distributed around V, while I_1 is symmetrically distributed around a fraction of V. Thus, σ_1 and σ_2 are measures for the possible range of the investment costs in each period. They can be interpreted as describing the degree of uncertainty. With this assumption, the first-order conditions from proposition 3.2 simplify to

$$I_1^* = q\,\frac{1}{8\sigma_2}[\sigma_2^2 - (V - I_2^*)^2] + \frac{\alpha}{2}V - \frac{\sigma_1}{2}, \tag{3.31}$$

$$I_2^* = V - 2\sigma_1 \frac{I_2^* - V + \sigma_2}{I_1^* - \alpha V + \sigma_1}. \tag{3.32}$$

An interesting question is, in what way the degree of uncertainty affects the critical investment values at t_1 and t_2. Since I_1^* and I_2^* interact, it is difficult to obtain a general answer even for uniformly distributed investment costs. The following proposition shows, how uncertainty affects the first period investment threshold.

Proposition 3.5. *If the investment costs I_1 and I_2 are distributed uniformly, the investment threshold I_1^* is decreasing in σ_1 and increasing in σ_2.*

Proposition 3.5 shows the ambiguous effect of an increasing uncertainty in both periods on the optimal investment threshold in the first period. While a higher uncertainty in the first period lowers the first-period investment threshold, it is increased by a higher second-period uncertainty. The reason is that higher uncertainty in the first period increases the information rent for the manager and hence causes headquarters to provide a more restrictive budget. In the second period, higher uncertainty makes the growth option more valuable. The option implies that the upside potential increases while the downside risk remains constant. Consequently, the second-period information rent for the manager increases and headquarters reduces the second-period budget to lower the information rent for the manager. The higher expected second-period value makes investment in the first period more attractive. Hence, the first-period investment threshold increases. Thus the investment threshold in the first period is affected by two different effects. On the one hand, the asymmetrically distributed information makes investment less attractive when uncertainty increases. On the other hand the opportunity to continue the project, i.e. the existence of the growth option, enhances the attractiveness of the project for increased uncertainty. Figure 3.2 shows this result for the parameter values $q = 1$, $V = 1$, $\alpha = 0.05$, and $\sigma_1 = 0.05$. The effect of uncertainty on the second period investment thresholds I_2^* can only be examined numerically. Such an analysis shows that for a wide range of parameter values, the second period investment threshold is decreasing in σ_2.

In this result two effects are combined. On the one hand, the (real) options literature has shown that increasing uncertainty makes investment more valuable, thus leading to an enhanced probability of investment. On the other hand, the literature on incentives in organizations has shown that increased uncertainty reduces the investment probability.[18] My result is a combination of these two effects showing the ambiguity of uncertainty on the investment thresholds in the case of a growth option.

[18] Here, I refer particularly to the result in Antle & Eppen (1985).

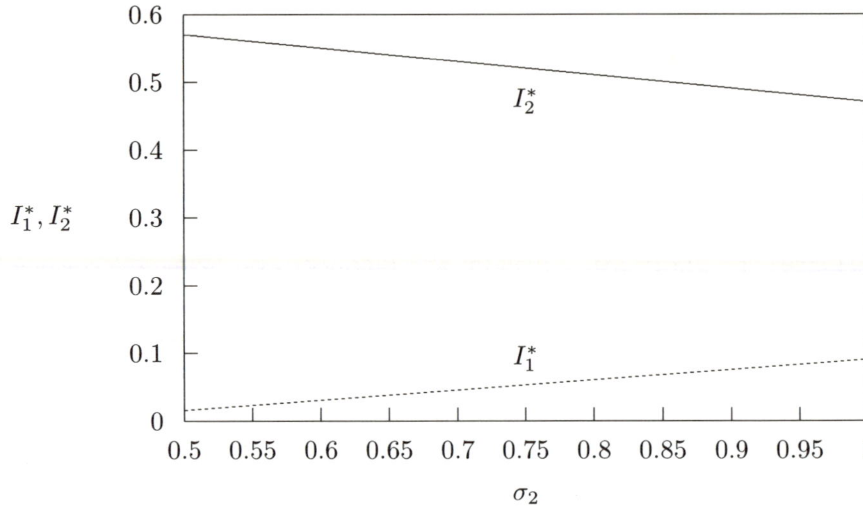

Fig. 3.2. Investment thresholds I_1^* and I_2^* as a function of σ_2

3.5 Implications for Capital Budgeting Procedures

In this chapter, I have analyzed managerial incentive problems, when investment opportunities have the form of a growth option and the manager has preference for slack. These conditions appear particularly in the context of R&D investments. The consulting business also partly fits into these conditions. Consider, e.g., the case, when the consultant as agent is conducting a two stage project for a client as principal and only completing both stages leads to a payoff for the client.

In solving my model, I have derived the optimal investment and budgeting strategies in this context. As in the first best world, the strategy consists of investment thresholds, below which investment takes place and above which no investment occurs. However, in both periods, the investment thresholds are lower compared to the first best case. The participation constraint is shown to have a significant effect on these investment thresholds. If the participation constraint is relaxed, the results get closer to first best. The reason is that the principal can use the manager's uncertainty about the investment cost of period two to extract her information rents from the period two investment.

This results can also be interpreted in terms of hurdle rates for investment decisions that have the form of a growth option. Comparing different participation constraints shows that higher hurdle rates are used, when participation constraints are more restrictive. If a manager is responsible only for a single project, rather the more restrictive participation constraints apply. This is the case, e.g., in small startups with only one project to develop. Thus, my model provides an additional explanation for the very high hurdle rates, that apply in financing decisions for startups. In contrast, consider a manager in a R&D division of a large firm. If she is responsible for the management of multiple projects, she would rather be able to shift excessive funds from one project to another. Hence, the participation constraint relaxes and the hurdle rates should be lower. My results indicate that the power of possible participation constraints should be carefully analyzed, when setting a hurdle rate for growth options.

In addition, my results provide an explanation of staging investment over time, i.e. splitting a single investment decision into several decisions that are made sequentially. Since new information arrives over time, the optimal investment path takes into account this new information. Staging investment instead of an upfront commitment to the whole investment project is the optimal response to information revelation over time. Interpreting this result in the area of entrepreneurial finance explains the widely observable behavior of several financing stages in venture capital investment[19] as well as corporate R&D investment.

The special case of uniformly distributed investment costs is used to analyze the effects of uncertainty on the investment thresholds. The results confirm the well known result from the real option literature that uncertainty can increase the value of an investment project. However, the investment thresholds are lower than in the first best world and, consequently, the probability of investment is lower. This result sheds some light on some anecdotal evidence that investment activities of firms investing in growth options like R&D are lower than real options models would suggest.[20] The literature on real options explains this observation by claiming that firms wrongly use the static net present value rule instead of a real options model. The static net present value rule leads to underinvestment for investment projects with embedded growth options.[21] Instead of this explanation, my results show that the existence of incentive problems provides reasons for this behavior. Firms have to limit the information rents associated with growth options and therefore forego some projects with positive value.

[19] See Neher (1999) for an explanation of staged financing in the face of a commitment problem using a model with perfect certainty.

[20] See Amram & Kulatilaka (1999), p. 168.

[21] See Friedl (2002a), pp. 73-81.

It is important to point out important restrictions of the model that might be a starting point for future research. First, I have assumed that slack is the only source of incentives for the manager. It would be interesting to analyze the case, when the manager is rewarded with a fraction of the principal's payoff. In this case, the principal has more degrees of freedom in designing an incentive scheme. That is particularly important, if there is an additional moral hazard problem. Second, in my model both parties are risk-neutral. A risk-averse agent would complicate the hidden information problem in our model. However, in many cases the assumption of risk-aversion seems to be more realistic. Third, I have picked out a special form of investment. Other real options could be added to this problem. In real life, investment projects usually contain several real options. The remainder of this work analyzes incentive issues for two different types of real options, namely the option to switch and the option to wait.

4

Residual Income as a Performance Measure for Switching Options

4.1 Residual Income-Based Performance Evaluation and Real Options

The last chapter analyzed capital rationing as an incentive device when information is asymmetrically distributed and growth options are present. The derived mechanism between headquarters and a manager was central in the sense that the manager reports her knowledge about investment costs to headquarters and the final investment decisions are made by headquarters. The underlying model structure seems to be reasonable for situations where the manager cannot or only marginally influence revenues, but has better information about costs as is the case for many R&D investment projects. From an organizational perspective, this kind of incentive device is likely to be more prevalent in companies that organize their activities in functional divisions along the value chain like for instance R&D, procurement, operations and sales.

In divisionalized companies with divisions being responsible for products or product lines and consequently for both cost and revenues and long-term consequences of decisions, capital rationing does not seem to be the appropriate mechanism, since it only affects the input side. In this organizational form, decision-making authority even for investment decisions is often delegated to divisional managers, who can influence both cost and revenues of their divisions. In order to induce the manager to make proper investment decisions, headquarters can rely on performance measures that motivate the manager to take the right actions. The present and the following chapter analyze situations, where investment decisions are completely delegated and headquarters uses performance-based compensation to induce the right actions.

The objective of this work is to analyze investment incentives, where investment has real options features. The set of available real options can strongly differ from situation to situation. While growth options and abandonment options are prevalent in the context of R&D, manufacturing decisions frequently involve the decision to switch from the production of one output to an alternative output. In order to explore the full range of different real options and the underlying decision situations, this chapter analyzes another real option, different from the growth option in the previous chapter. I use the case of investment in a flexible manufacturing system to analyze the incentive properties of residual income in the presence of real options. A flexible manufacturing system provides the flexibility to switch from one output to an alternative output, if conditions change. This flexibility creates additional value that is not included in the basic value of the original production plan. This additional value is the option to switch.[1]

Among the set of possible performance measures, I restrict myself on the analysis of incentives provided by residual income based performance measures. The reason for this confinement is twofold.[2] First, starting from practical experience and empirical evidence[3], a growing number of firms has started to use residual income as a performance measure for managers. Consulting firms have helped to popularize this concept under different labels, the most popular of which is probably the concept of Economic Value Added (EVA).[4] Second, parallel to this development, the academic literature came up with strong support for the use of residual income as a performance measure. Numerous papers showed that residual income has advantages compared to alternative performance measures such as income or cash flows.[5]

This chapter addresses the question, if the strong incentive properties of residual income still hold for the case when real options are present. There is at least some anecdotal evidence that this is not the case. Performance measures based on residual income are often suspected to support short-term orientation of the management and hamper managerial decisions that are beneficial only in the long run. One way, practitioners deal with this problem is the implementation of bonus

[1] See Margrabe (1978) and Carr (1988) for the valuation of the option to switch in a single-person decision context.

[2] See also the discussion in section 2.2.3.

[3] See Pellens, et al. (1998).

[4] See, e.g., Ehrbar (1998); Stern et al. (2001); Young & O'Byrne (2001).

[5] See particularly Rogerson (1997); Reichelstein (1997). See also Baldenius (2002); Dutta & Reichelstein (1999); Dutta & Reichelstein (2002b); Dutta & Reichelstein (2002a); Pfeiffer (2000); Reichelstein (2000); Wagenhofer (2003).

banks, i.e. compensation based on residual income is not paid instantly, but with a time-lag up to several years.[6]

In the last chapter I used a principal-agent model to analyze the capital rationing problem for growth options. Due to the dynamic modelling of the adverse selection problem, a lot of purely technical issues arose. Since the performance evaluation problem is even more complex, it appears to be reasonable to use a simplified approach for the analysis of the performance evaluation problem. I therefore use a goal congruence model[7] to evaluate alternative residual income based performance measures. This type of model is in line with a large part of the existing literature.[8] A drawback of these models is the fact that compensation payments to the manager are neglected in the objective function of headquarters. The advantage on the other hand is that the results are relatively robust against changes in the exact specifications of the agent's utility or distributional assumptions.[9]

The model in this chapter contributes to the existing literature in several ways. First and most importantly, the existing literature on the optimality of residual income as a performance measure does not consider the arrival of new information after investment has been made. Only recently some work on incentive issues in the presence of managerial flexibility has been done.[10] I show that the existing framework for the design of residual income as a performance measure must be extended to create goal congruence in the presence of real options. Second, the literature on real options has almost entirely focused on valuation issues in a single-person decision context. I demonstrate, how to design performance measures that create incentives for managers to exercise this real options in a value-maximizing way.

The remainder of the chapter is organized as follows. In the next section, I describe a model of investment in a flexible manufacturing system and the objectives of the manager and headquarters. Section

---

[6] See, e.g., Young & O'Byrne (2001), pp. 147-158.

[7] See section 2.3.3.

[8] See Rogerson (1997); Reichelstein (1997); Dutta & Reichelstein (2002a).

[9] See section 2.3.3 for a detailed discussion.

[10] For example, Antle et al. (2000) and chapter 3 analyze agency models, where the manager has private information about an investment with an embedded real option. However, they analyze capital budgeting issues and do not consider residual income as a performance measure. Dutta & Reichelstein (2002a) analyze residual income as a performance measure for research and development investments, when the project can be abandoned before it generates cash inflows. Dutta (2003) analyzes residual income as a managerial performance measure, when the manager can invest in a growth opportunity that can also be implemented outside the firm.

4.3 analyzes and discusses different design alternatives for the residual income performance measure in the presence of a switching option. Section 4.4 provides two other applications. Section 4.5 considers some implications.

4.2 Modelling Investment in a Flexible Manufacturing System

4.2.1 Model Setup

My model consists of headquarters and a single divisional manager who is responsible for investment decisions in an investment center. Headquarters delegates an investment project to a manager who is better informed about the project. The class of investment projects I consider consists of two sequential decisions. The first decision is the immediate investment decision that cannot be postponed.[11] The second decision is the decision to switch from the originally manufactured product to an alternative product and can only be made at time $t = \tau$ with $1 < \tau < T$. I assume that each decision is contingent on the realization of a random variable that is only known to the manager at the time of decision. There are two possibly multidimensional random variables, $\tilde{\theta}_0$ and $\tilde{\theta}_\tau$, corresponding to the two decisions.

The first investment requires an initial cash outlay b_0 at $t = 0$, and has cash inflows of $\{c_{0,1}, ..., c_{0,\tau}\}$, where $c_{0,t} = x_{0,t} \cdot f_0(\theta_0)$, $x_{0,t} \geq 0$ and $f_0(\theta_0) > 0$. The distributional parameter $x_{0,t}$, which reflects the distribution of cash flows over time, is assumed to be commonly known to both, the manager and headquarters. For instance, they both might know that the cash flows are constant over time, which results in constant distributional parameters over time. However the manager has private information about the profitability of the project, given by the function $f_0(\theta_0)$. For example, she might be better informed about market prices or production costs than headquarters. At time $t = \tau$, the random variable $\tilde{\theta}_\tau$ realizes. Now the firm can either continue producing the original product or switch to an alternative product. In the former case, the cash flows are determined by $c_{\tau,\tau+1}, ..., c_{\tau,T}$, where $c_{\tau,t} = x_{\tau,t} \cdot f_\tau(\theta_\tau)$, $x_{\tau,t} \geq 0$ and $f_\tau(\theta_\tau) > 0$. In the latter case, the decision to switch requires an initial cash investment b_τ at $t = \tau$, and leads to subsequent cash inflows of $c^s_{\tau,\tau+1}, ..., c^s_{\tau,T}$, where $c^s_{\tau,t} = x_{\tau,t} \cdot g_\tau(\theta_\tau)$, and $g_\tau(\theta_\tau) > 0$. In both cases, $x_{\tau,t}$ again is a distributional parameter. Note that I assume identical

[11] A natural extension of this assumption would be to allow for a timing option, i.e. investment can be postponed. Chapter 5 analyzes this case.

distributional parameters for both alternatives. This assumption seems reasonable in cases, when the capacity limit determines the amount of output, since the capacity constraint applies for both kinds of products. Both $f_\tau(\theta_\tau)$ and $g_\tau(\theta_\tau)$ are increasing functions of a random variable that determines the profitability of the two alternatives. At the time the first investment decision is made, both share common beliefs on the distribution of the random variables. At $t = \tau$, just before the switching decision has to be made, the manager privately observes the realization of θ_τ.

The value of investment at time $t = \tau$ therefore is

$$V_\tau(\theta_\tau) = \max\{ \sum_{t=\tau+1}^{T} x_{\tau,t} \cdot f_\tau(\theta_\tau) \cdot \gamma^{t-\tau}, -b_\tau + \sum_{t=\tau+1}^{T} x_{\tau,t} \cdot g_\tau(\theta_\tau) \cdot \gamma^{t-\tau}\} \tag{4.1}$$

where $\gamma = 1/(1+r)$ is headquarters' discount factor and r is the company's cost of capital. The option-like characteristic of this decision comes from the fact that there is a right but no obligation to switch from the original product to an alternative product. This right can be acquired by investing into the flexible manufacturing system. The overall value of investment then becomes

$$V_0(\theta_0) = -b_0 + \sum_{t=1}^{\tau} x_{0,t} \cdot f_0(\theta_0) \cdot \gamma^t + \gamma^\tau \cdot E_{\theta_\tau}[V_\tau(\tilde{\theta}_\tau)] \tag{4.2}$$

Note that $\gamma^\tau \cdot E_{\theta_\tau}[V_\tau(\tilde{\theta}_\tau)] \geq 0$, i.e. at $t = 0$, the expected value of the second stage is always nonnegative, since I have assumed nonnegative distributional parameters.

4.2.2 Headquarters' Objective

To set the benchmark, I state the decision rules for the switching decision and the initial investment decision from headquarters' point of view. Under the net present value rule, headquarters wants to switch, if and only if

$$-b_\tau + \sum_{t=\tau+1}^{T} x_{\tau,t} \cdot g_\tau(\theta_\tau) \cdot \gamma^{t-\tau} \geq \sum_{t=\tau+1}^{T} x_{\tau,t} \cdot f_\tau(\theta_\tau) \cdot \gamma^{t-\tau}. \tag{4.3}$$

Similarly, headquarters wants to invest at $t = 0$, if and only if

$$V_0(\theta_0) = -b_0 + \sum_{t=1}^{\tau} x_{0,t} \cdot f_0(\theta_0) \cdot \gamma^t + \gamma^\tau \cdot E_{\theta_\tau}[V_\tau(\tilde{\theta}_\tau)] \geq 0. \qquad (4.4)$$

In this expression, the value of the usual net present value rule is extended by the value of the second stage. The value of the switching option SO at $t = 0$ is the difference between the value at the second stage and the value of the original product in the second stage:

$$SO = \gamma^\tau \cdot E_{\theta_\tau} \left[V_\tau(\tilde{\theta}_\tau) - \sum_{t=\tau+1}^{T} x_{\tau,t} \cdot f_\tau(\theta_\tau) \cdot \gamma^{t-\tau} \right].$$

4.2.3 Goal Congruence and Manager's Objective

In my model, not headquarters, but the better informed divisional manager makes the investment decisions. To make investment decisions according to headquarters' objective, she must be given the right incentives. That can be done by basing her compensation on performance measures that reflect the results of her investment activities. If a performance measure creates incentives for the manager to invest in projects according to headquarters' objective, the measure is said to be goal congruent. In my model of investment in the presence of real options, goal congruence requires that the manager's investment strategy at both times of decision is in line with headquarters' objectives.

The analysis focuses on residual income based performance measures. Residual income RI_t in period t is defined as the difference between accounting income Inc_t and a capital charge calculated with interest rate r for the value of the assets in place, V_{t-1}:[12]

$$RI_t = Inc_t - r \cdot V_{t-1}$$

Given residual income as a performance measure and restricting the set of possible contracts to be linear in the performance measure, the manager's objective is to maximize her utility U from future compensation payments. I assume that the manager maximizes the expected discounted value of her bonus payments:

$$U = E_{\theta_\tau} \left[\sum_{t=1}^{T} \delta^t \cdot k \cdot RI_t(\tilde{\theta}_\tau) \right]$$

[12] For a detailed description see section 2.2.3.

where k is the linear bonus parameter[13] and $\delta = 1/(1 + r_M)$ is the manager's discount factor for future compensation payments. I assume $\delta \leq \gamma$. If $\delta = \gamma$, the discount factors of headquarters and the manager are the same. A smaller discount factor of the manager implies, that she uses a higher interest rate r_M to discount future compensation payments and hence has stronger preferences for sooner payments. In line with the literature on goal congruent performance measures, it is reasonable to assume that the manager's interest rate is higher than the company's. In this case, the manager is said to be impatient. One reason could be that with positive probability, the manager leaves the firm or her position before all benefits of the investment have been realized. Then the manager does not benefit from parts of the project. Another reason could be that capital markets are imperfect, and the manager has not the same access to the capital market as the company.

4.3 Design Alternatives for the Residual Income Performance Measure

So far I was not specific about the calculation of the residual income performance measure. There are several degrees of freedom in designing this measure. I distinguish between a myopic accounting system and an adjusted accounting system, which is able to record the option value of the switching option. The myopic accounting system allows for flexible depreciation schedules but requires all investment outlays being fully depreciated in the time period of the directly induced cash flows. The adjusted accounting system also allows for flexible depreciation schedules. However, the depreciation schedule is not required to fully depreciate the total investment outlays in the time period of directly induced cash flows.

4.3.1 Myopic Accounting Rules

A myopic accounting system consists of a depreciation schedule for each cash investment and a capital charge rate. For the initial investment, the depreciation schedule is determined by $\{d_{0,t}\}_{t=1}^{\tau}$, where the depreciation in each period is $d_{0,t} \cdot b_0$, $1 \leq t \leq \tau$ and $\sum_{t=1}^{\tau} d_{0,t} = 1$. When the manager receives new information in $t = \tau$, the depreciation schedule for the

[13] In fact, all results in this chapter also hold for nonlinear compensation functions. The only requirement is that in each period, the manager's compensation is an increasing function of residual income.

second stage becomes $\{d_{\tau,t}\}_{t=\tau+1}^{T}$. If the manager continues with the original product, the depreciation in each period is 0, while it is $d_{\tau,t} \cdot b_\tau$ with $\sum_{t=\tau+1}^{T} d_{\tau,t} = 1$, if the manager decides to switch for $\tau+1 \leq t \leq T$. The residual income in each period of the first τ periods is

$$RI_t = c_{0,t} - d_{0,t} \cdot b_0 - r \cdot B_{0,t-1},$$

while from period $\tau + 1$, residual income depends on the decision to switch:

$$RI_t = \begin{cases} c_{\tau,t} & \text{if no switching} \\ c_{\tau,t}^s - d_{\tau,t} \cdot b_\tau - r \cdot B_{\tau,t-1} & \text{if switching} \end{cases}$$

Here $B_{i,t-1} = B_{i,t} + d_{i,t} \cdot b_i$, $i \in \{0, \tau\}$ is the value of the nondepreciated parts of the investment at time $t-1$ with $B_{i,i} = b_i$ and $B_{i,t-1} = b_i(1 - \sum_{j=i+1}^{t-1} d_{i,j})$.

The total charges $z_{0,t} \cdot b_0$ are the sum of depreciation and capital charges and for each period given by

$$z_{0,t} \cdot b_0 = d_{0,t} \cdot b_0 + r \cdot B_{0,t-1} = b_0 \left[d_{0,t} + r \cdot (1 - \sum_{j=1}^{t-1} d_{0,j})\right]$$

for the initial periods $1 \leq t \leq \tau$ and

$$z_{\tau,t} \cdot b_\tau = d_{\tau,t} \cdot b_\tau + r \cdot B_{\tau,t-1} = b_\tau \left[d_{\tau,t} + r \cdot (1 - \sum_{j=\tau+1}^{t-1} d_{\tau,j})\right]$$

for the switching periods $\tau+1 \leq t \leq T$. Suppose now that both investment stages are independent of each other. That is, the second decision, when the manager has to choose between the two alternatives, can be made even if the first investment has not been made. Contrary, the first investment does not contain an option to switch. In this case, residual income is the unique optimal performance measure, provided depreciation is calculated according to the relative benefit depreciation schedule.[14] The relative benefit depreciation schedule distributes depreciation over the useful life of a project in a way that the sum of depreciation and capital charges in each period is equal to the relative weight of the cash flow value of that period.[15] Thus the periodical charges are

[14] For the first decision, this result follows immediately from proposition 3 in Reichelstein (1997), p. 168. The second decision can be considered as a mutually exclusive investment opportunity, and a derivation of a corresponding result is straightforward for our assumption of identically distributed cash flows.

[15] See Rogerson (1997).

$$z_{0,t} = \frac{x_{0,t}}{\sum_{j=1}^{\tau} x_{0,j}\, \gamma^j}, \tag{4.5}$$

and

$$z_{\tau,t} = \frac{x_{\tau,t}}{\sum_{j=\tau+1}^{T} x_{\tau,j}\, \gamma^{j-\tau}}, \tag{4.6}$$

respectively. Residual income in period t as a function of the profitability parameters θ_0 and θ_τ for the first and the second stage therefore becomes

$$RI_t(\theta_0) = c_{0,t} - z_{0,t} \cdot b_0 \quad \text{if} \quad 1 \leq t \leq \tau$$

$$RI_t(\tilde{\theta}_\tau) = \begin{cases} c_{\tau,t} & \text{if no switching,} \\ & \text{and } \tau + 1 \leq t \leq T \\ c^s_{\tau,t} - d_{\tau,t} \cdot b_\tau - r \cdot B_{\tau,t-1} & \text{if switching,} \\ & \text{and } \tau + 1 \leq t \leq T \end{cases}$$

Given the form of the manager's utility function with residual income calculated as above, in general goal congruence can only be achieved for special cases, as the following proposition shows. (See the appendix for details and a proof)

Proposition 4.1. *1. If the manager discounts future benefits at a higher rate than headquarters ($\delta < \gamma$), then myopic accounting rules always lead to underinvestment for the initial investment decision in the presence of a switching option.*

2. If the discount factor of headquarters and the manager is identical, the residual income performance measure based on myopic accounting rules is a goal congruent performance measure in the presence of a switching option.

3. Myopic accounting rules always achieve goal congruence for the switching decision.

The first part of the proposition shows that an impatient manager always underinvests under myopic accounting rules, if there is an option to switch. The intuitive reason for this result is that myopic accounting rules do not consider the option value, which is a consequence of the initial investment decision. Even if the manager recognizes the option value and its consequences for the future performance measures, he discounts this benefits at a higher rate than headquarters. Therefore, he puts less weight on the option value than headquarters would do, which results in underinvestment.

If headquarters and the manager have identical discount factors, goal congruence can be achieved by a myopic residual income measure even in the presence of real options. The reason simply is that with identical discount factors, discounting residual income results in the same valuation as discounting cash flows.[16]

For the last stage decision, goal congruence is always achieved by myopic accounting rules, since this decision is independent of additional future decisions. Therefore, this decision is effectively equal to a case, where the manager faces a mutually exclusive investment opportunity without embedded real options.

4.3.2 Recording the Option Value

The last section has shown that in general a myopic accounting system cannot achieve goal congruence. A natural question to ask is whether the accounting system can properly be adjusted to allow for the construction of a performance measure that achieves goal congruence even for investment decisions with embedded real options. This kind of investment decisions differ from ordinary investment decisions in two respects that have to be considered for performance measurement. First, in exchange for the initial cash outlay, the company not only gets a stream of cash flows, but also a real option with an uncertain value. Second, the assumption of a commonly known overall distribution of cash flows over time cannot hold in the presence of real options. Even if the distribution of cash flows is known for each part of the investment decision, the same cannot be true for the overall distribution. The reason is that the value of the option to switch is uncertain to both the manager as well as headquarters. Therefore, it is impossible to calculate the relative weight of this investment opportunity compared to the stream of cash flows of the initial investment, which are also uncertain from headquarter's point of view but with a possibly different level. However this weight is necessary in order to properly allocate the initial investment outlays on the following periods.

I now analyze, if an alternative slightly more general accounting system is able to create a residual income performance measure that achieves goal congruence. In contrast to the previous section, I drop the requirement for the depreciation schedule to fully depreciate the investment outlay during the time period of the directly induced cash flows. Thus I allow for the possibility that only parts of the initial investment outlay have to be depreciated. As a consequence, the depreciation charges for the initial investment become $d_{0,t} \cdot (b_0 - \Gamma_0)$, where

[16] This result is the well-known Preinreich-Luecke-Theorem, see Preinreich (1937) and Lücke (1955).

Γ_0 is a parameter, which reduces the amount to be depreciated. Alternatively, this procedure can be interpreted as capitalizing the value Γ_0 at the time investment is made. The capital charges must also reflect this proceeding. They have to be calculated based on $\hat{B}_0$ where $\hat{B}_{0,t-1} = \hat{B}_{0,t} + d_{0,t} \cdot (b_0 - \Gamma_0)$ and $\hat{B}_{0,0} = b_0 - \Gamma_0$. With the so defined depreciation schedule, the total charges from the initial investment for period $t \geq 1$ become

$$\begin{aligned} z_{0,t} \cdot (b_0 - \Gamma_0) &= d_{0,t} \cdot (b_0 - \Gamma_0) + r \cdot \hat{B}_{0,t-1} \\ &= (b_0 - \Gamma_0) \left[d_{0,t} + r \cdot \left(1 - \sum_{j=1}^{t-1} d_{0,j} \right) \right] \end{aligned}$$

Suppose, the periodic charges for the initial investment are again chosen according to the relative benefit depreciation schedule, so that the periodic charges match the time value of cash flows:

$$z_{0,t} = \frac{x_{0,t}}{\sum_{j=1}^{T} x_{0,j}\, \gamma^j}$$

At the time, the switching decision is made, the option has expired and is therefore left valueless, regardless whether it has been exercised or not. I therefore allow for an additional positive value Γ_τ to be depreciated during the periods following $t = \tau$. Hence the total charges from the second decision become

$$\begin{aligned} z_{\tau,t} \cdot (b_\tau + \Gamma_\tau) &= d_{\tau,t}\, \Gamma_\tau + r\, \hat{B}_{\tau,t-1} \quad \text{if no switching} \\ z_{\tau,t} \cdot (b_\tau + \Gamma_\tau) &= d_{\tau,t}\, (b_\tau + \Gamma_\tau) + r\, \hat{B}^s_{\tau,t-1} \quad \text{if switching} \end{aligned}$$

where $\hat{B}_{\tau,t-1} = \hat{B}_{\tau,t} + d_{\tau,t} \cdot \Gamma_\tau$ with $\hat{B}_{\tau,\tau} = \Gamma_\tau$, and $\hat{B}^s_{\tau,t-1} = \hat{B}^s_{\tau,t} + d_{\tau,t} \cdot (b_\tau - \Gamma_\tau)$ with $\hat{B}^s_{\tau,\tau} = b_\tau - \Gamma_\tau$. The periodic charges are again assumed to be chosen as to accomplish the relative benefit depreciation rule:

$$z_{\tau,t} = \frac{x_{\tau,t}}{\sum_{j=\tau+1}^{T} x_{\tau,j}\, \gamma^{j-\tau}}.$$

Now suppose, Γ_0 is chosen as to equal the discounted expected value of the investment at the time the switching decision has to be made, and Γ_τ is chosen as to equal the same value compounded at headquarters' rate until date τ:

$$\begin{aligned} \Gamma_0 &= \gamma^\tau\, E_{\theta_\tau}[V_\tau(\tilde{\theta}_\tau)] \\ \Gamma_\tau &= E_{\theta_\tau}[V_\tau(\tilde{\theta}_\tau)] \end{aligned}$$

In this case the residual income measure achieves goal congruence for both decisions. I state this result in the following proposition:[17]

Proposition 4.2. *A performance measure based on residual income achieves goal congruence for investment decisions with an embedded option to switch, if*

1. *the option value is capitalized and subsequently depreciated, and*
2. *the structure of the periodic depreciation charges is calculated according to the relative benefit depreciation schedule.*

This proposition shows that with an adjustment of the accounting system residual income remains a goal congruent performance measure for investments with embedded switching options. The accounting system has to depreciate only parts of the initial investment outlay, namely, the initial cash outlay less the expected value of the second stage including the switching option. At the time the exercise of the option to switch has to be decided, the compounded value of this stage must be depreciated in addition to a possible switching cost. This accounting procedure can also be interpreted as capitalizing the discounted expected value of the second stage, if investment is undertaken in the first stage. Doing that, the accounting system effectively separates the first investment decision, where the manager has some private information, from the second decision, where uncertainty is distributed symmetrically among the manager and headquarters. This separation leads to a goal congruent solution for both investment decisions.

4.3.3 Discussion of Recording the Option Value

The proposed accounting system for managerial performance evaluation in the case of investments with embedded switching options differs from previously discussed systems in one important attribute. It does not need to have a completely tidy depreciation schedule, i.e., the sum of depreciations has not necessarily to be equal to the total amount of invested capital. This property results from the fact that parts of the total depreciation amount are shifted to a later date. By doing so, the nondepreciated parts have to be compounded up to the time, they are depreciated.[18] The requirement of "tidiness" frequently results from external accounting rules. However, there is no reason to transfer

[17] Details and a formal proof are provided in the appendix.

[18] The sum of total depreciation over both stages is $\sum_{t=1}^{\tau} d_{0,t}\,(b_0 - \Gamma_0) + \sum_{t=\tau+1}^{T} d_{\tau,t}\,(b_\tau + \Gamma_\tau) = b_0 + b_\tau - \Gamma_0 + \Gamma_\tau = b_0 + b_\tau + E_{\theta_\tau}[V_\tau(\tilde{\theta}_\tau)]\,(1 - \gamma)$.

this requirement also to an internal accounting system, in particular for performance evaluation purposes. If goal congruence for investment decisions is required, the design of the accounting system should follow this objective and should not stick to tidy depreciation schedules.

A more serious problem arises at the time, the exercise decision has to be made. At this point, the compounded expected value that has not been depreciated so far, lowers future residual incomes. Though being goal congruent, this accounting treatment can cause different problems. For instance, if the realization of the true state θ_T is below expectations, the manager sees herself confronted with a series of negative future residual incomes. She therefore might well be tempted to simply leave the firm. If headquarters wants to keep the manager, the compensation rule has to be changed. But then a manager anticipating this kind of headquarters' behavior has incentives to deviate from goal congruent investment decision.

The proposed accounting rules also raise the question of the danger of manipulating the option value from the manager's point of view. Only if headquarters has a reliable expectation about the option value that is equal to the manager's, the proposed accounting rules are adequate. If on the other hand the manager has private information about the option value, the performance measure has to take into account the different information structure. It is at least questionable, whether residual income remains a goal congruent performance measure in this situation.

There are two crucial information requirements, if headquarters wants to achieve goal congruence with residual income as a performance measure. At the time of the first stage investment, it has to know the distribution of cash flows from the first investment in order to be able to calculate the periodical depreciation and capital charges according to the relative benefit depreciation schedule. It also must have expectations about the value of the switching option that are identical with the manager's. At the time of the first investment, headquarters does not need to know the distribution of cash flows of the second stage of investment. However, this information becomes a necessary ingredient at the time of investing in the second stage.

This informational requirements are not so demanding as they might seem. If a flexible manufacturing system operates at its capacity limit, the distribution of future cash flows might well be assessable by considering the amount of produced and sold goods. The manager in contrast might have superior information with respect to the contribution margin of a single product. However this superior information might not apply for the option value, since other types of uncertainty might determine the option value, which can be assessed by headquarters as well.

4.4 Applying the Results to Different Types of Real Options

So far I have considered the case of investment in a flexible manufacturing system with an embedded option to switch. The considerations in this chapter can also be used to design a goal congruent performance measure for other types of real options.

The structural analogy is that in each case, the initial investment decision allows for an additional decision at a later point in time, when uncertainty resolves. To demonstrate the principle, I use two examples, a strategic investment decision that includes a growth option and therefore is similar to the case considered in the previous chapter and the acquisition of a company implemented by an option contract.

4.4.1 Strategic Investment Decisions

A strategic investment enables a firm to make an additional investment at a later point in time, once the initial investment has been made. The value of the additional investment depends on the realization of an uncertain state variable. The additional investment will only be made, if the realization of the state variable is favorable. Formally, the initial investment is b_0, and the stream of cash flows induced by the initial investment is $\{x_{0,t} \cdot f_0(\theta_0)\}_{t=1}^{T}$. At $t = \tau$, the firm has the option to make an additional investment with initial cash outlays b_τ and a stream of additional cash flows $\{x_{\tau,t} \cdot f_\tau(\theta_\tau)\}_{t=\tau+1}^{T}$. At $t = 0$, both headquarters and the manager have identical expectations on the state variable, while at $t = \tau$, the manager privately learns its true value. At time $t = \tau$, when uncertainty resolves, the value of the additional cash flows of the strategic investment is

$$V_\tau(\theta_\tau) = \max\{-b_\tau + \sum_{t=\tau+1}^{T} x_{\tau,t} \cdot f_\tau(\theta_\tau) \cdot \gamma^{t-\tau}, 0\}$$

The value of the initial cash flows is not affected by this decision. Hence, the overall value of the strategic investment at $t = 0$ is

$$V_0(\theta_0) = -b_0 + \sum_{t=1}^{T} x_{0,t} \cdot f_0(\theta_0) \cdot \gamma^t + \gamma^\tau \cdot E_{\theta_\tau}[V_\tau(\tilde{\theta}_\tau)]$$

which is the same as equation (4.2) except the last term that is now the value of the second stage of the strategic investment, and the second term on the right-hand side, which includes cash flows until $t = T$. From headquarters point of view, it is optimal to invest in the second stage, if and only if

$$-b_\tau + \sum_{t=\tau+1}^{T} x_{\tau,t} \cdot f_\tau(\theta_\tau) \cdot \gamma^{t-\tau} \geq 0$$

i.e. if the net present value of the second stage is nonnegative. First stage investment is optimal if and only if $V_0(\theta_0) \geq 0$. However, the manager maximizes the value of his compensation payments based on the performance measure and discounted at $\delta < \gamma$. It is now straightforward to verify that a residual income performance measure based on the proposed adjusted accounting rules achieves goal congruence. For the first investment stage, the total amount to be depreciated is the difference between the initial investment outlay b_0 and the discounted option value of the additional investment $\gamma^\tau \cdot E_{\theta_\tau}[V_\tau(\tilde{\theta}_\tau)]$. Again, depreciation has to be calculated according to the relative benefit depreciation schedule. The total amount to be depreciated at the second stage is the sum of the original expected value of this stage, $E_{\theta_\tau}[V_\tau(\tilde{\theta}_\tau)]$, and b_τ, should investment take place. If no additional investment takes place, only the value of the growth option has to be depreciated. Now depreciation has to be calculated according to the relative benefit depreciation schedule, based on the distribution of cash flows induced by the second stage investment.

4.4.2 Business Acquisitions

Business acquisitions are frequently implemented by an option contract. The buyer of a target acquires only a certain share in connection with the option to acquire the remaining share at or until a given future date. Obviously, the buyer will only exercise the option, if the strike price is lower than the sum of expected discounted cash flows from the remaining shares. Suppose that the manager who is in charge of the acquisition is better informed about the value of cash flows and potential synergies in each period, while headquarters is able to estimate their distribution over time. Furthermore, suppose that exercising the option depends on the resolution of some state variable which is uncertain to both, the manager and headquarters. Then the initial cash investment is the buying price for a defined share of the target at $t = 0$, represented by b_0. The cash flows belonging to this share are $\{x_{0,t} \cdot f_0(\theta_0)\}_{t=1}^{T}$. The present value of the option to acquire the whole target at $t = \tau$ with strike price b_τ is $\gamma^\tau \cdot E_{\theta_\tau}[V_\tau(\tilde{\theta}_\tau)]$. The cash flows associated with the remaining share of the target are $\{x_{\tau,t} \cdot f_\tau(\theta_\tau)\}_{t=\tau+1}^{T}$.

Now this situation is formally identical to the case of strategic investment discussed in the last subsection. Therefore, a goal congruent performance measure depreciates the difference between the initial buying price and the value of the option at the time of buying, and distributes depreciation according to the relative benefit depreciation schedule. At the exercise time of the option, the sum of the compounded initial option value and the strike price, should the option be exercised, will be depreciated. Since my result is independent of the book value of assets of the acquired company, the existence of goodwill does not change the results.[19] Put it differently, the depreciation schedule has to be applied to the sum of the book value of the existing assets and goodwill according to the acquired share less the compounded option value.

This two applications provide some general insights how to modify the residual income performance measure, when real options are present and the option value can be calculated from both headquarters and the manager. The option value has simply to be subtracted from the initial cash outlays and reduces the amount to be depreciated. When uncertainty resolves, the compounded option value has to be depreciated over the remaining useful life of the project as if the option were exercised.

4.5 Implications for the Design of the Residual Income Performance Measure

The objective of this chapter was to analyze residual income as a managerial performance measure in the presence of real options. With an important modification in the accounting system, residual income is shown to provide goal congruent investment incentives. The modification takes into account the option value of a project and removes this value from the initial decision for depreciation purposes. The compounded capitalized value will be depreciated beginning with the period of the decision to exercise the option. Doing that, the accounting system effectively separates the two interlinked decisions and is therefore able to give incentives on a period-by-period basis.

Although the chapter provides some general insights regarding the accounting treatment of real options, still a lot of work remains to

[19] See Corona (2002) for a detailed analysis of a goal congruent treatment of goodwill in business acquisitions, when residual income is used for managerial performance evaluation.

be done in this area. For instance, the literature on real options usually considers gradually resolving uncertainty that follows stochastic processes.[20] In contrast, this chapter examines a situation with a sudden realization of an uncertain state variable. An analysis of incentive issues in the context of gradually resolving uncertainty might be an interesting topic for future research. Another extension could aim on explaining the frequently observable behavior of asset write-downs when or shortly after a manager is replaced. This chapter sheds some light on this issue from the perspective of uncertain investments with embedded real options. A bad realization of a state variable leaves the current manager with the prospect of negative future compensation payments, so that he is likely to leave the firm. To prevent a new manager from starting with the prospect of negative compensation payments, either the compensation rules have to be changed, or write-downs are necessary. Finally, I have not considered the option to wait that plays an important role in corporate practice as well as in the literature. This option comes with additional difficulties, since accounting for it has to start when there is a valuable option to wait, even at a time when no investment has taken place yet. Therefore the next chapter analyzes managerial investment incentive issues in the presence of an option to wait.

[20] See, e.g., Friedl (2000).

5

Residual Income as a Performance Measure in the Presence of Waiting Options

5.1 Relevance of Waiting Options for Investment Decisions

So far I have analyzed real options that are available only if an initial investment has been made. A growth option requires investment in a first stage, which is necessary to open the opportunity for a subsequent investment. In order to be able to exercise a switching option, it is necessary to previously having invested in a flexible production facility. A different type of a real option is the option to wait. This option does not necessarily require an initial investment. It is available, when an investment opportunity exists that can be postponed. Postponement of a project is often an option that proves to be valuable in situations with huge uncertainty. There are many situations, when this option to wait is of practical importance. The exploration and development of natural resources with uncertain spot prices is a prominent example.[1] Further examples include the timing of a market entry with uncertain demand, the timing of adoption of a new technology, or the timing of starting a new business.[2] Moreover, for many major investment projects it is quite common to postpone the final decision, if the arrival of valuable new information is expected that can alter the final decision.

When considering the properties of residual income with respect to giving investment incentives, the theoretical literature has mainly taken the following view. At each point in time, there is a set of investment opportunities, in general not mutually exclusive, and the manager can pick the project she likes and leave the projects undone she does not

[1] See, e.g., Ekern (1988); Paddock, et al. (1988); Smit (1997).

[2] For these and further applications see Copeland & Antikarov (2001).

like. Once a project is rejected, the opportunity is gone forever.[3] Of course, this simple view does not meet reality at all and conflicts with the notion of waiting options. As illustrated by the above examples, in many situations an available project can be carried out either now or later. In particular

Only recently some authors have started to develop models of asymmetric information that include investment decisions with the option to postpone a project. The pioneering work has been done by Antle et al. (2000) who derived an optimal contract in a two-period adverse selection model with a timing option. Chapter 3 analyzes a similar model for a single investment decision that includes a growth option. Due to the complexity of these models, and since their focus is on capital budgeting, they do not explicitly give recommendations with respect to performance measures. Their investment policy is characterized by hurdle rates that determine the investment threshold. Arya & Glover (2001) also analyze a situation with a timing option in the presence of incentive problems. In their model, an incentive problem makes the option to wait valuable when it would not have been valuable otherwise. Stark (2000) considers the option to wait and the option to abandon a project when residual income is used as a performance measure. He makes the point that the accounting system must record the value of the option to wait. Using the same performance measure, Crasselt (2003a) analyzes different options, including a timing option.[4] For his set of assumptions, he comes up with the fairly pessimistic conclusion that "it is generally impossible for the owner to create an incentive scheme that does not give the manager any incentives to deviate from the first-best investment strategy if the investment decision has real options features." Contrary to this finding, I show that in my setting with a timing option, it is relatively straightforward to obtain two different forms of goal congruent residual income measures.

This chapter continues and extends the existing work on combined issues of the valuation of the option to wait and the analysis of performance measures for investment decision making. Interestingly, it shows that using residual income calculated according to a simple depreciation policy leads to a wrong exercise of the timing option. The manager will invest to early, which is a form of overinvestment. This result in the context of waiting options contrasts to the result in the previous chapter that suggests underinvestment in the presence of switching options. As a consequence, it seems to be important to exactly specify the nature of

[3] For this assumption see Rogerson (1997) and Reichelstein (1997).
[4] See also Crasselt (2003b).

real options associated with investment projects to draw robust conclusions on managerial investment behavior in the presence of real options. Moreover, this chapter shows that residual income, if properly adjusted, can be a goal congruent performance measure even in the presence of a waiting option. If a manager, who discounts future benefits possibly at a different rate than the owners of a firm, is compensated based on residual income, she will carry out exactly the same investment policy as headquarters if it were perfectly informed. However, the residual income measure has to be carefully designed with respect to the capitalization and depreciation rules as well as the capital charge rate. Two alternative approaches are suggested. The first alternative depreciates not only the initial investment outlay, but also the value of the option to wait, regardless whether the option is exercised now or later. Furthermore, if the option expires without being exercised, its value has to be depreciated at the time of expiration.[5] The second alternative uses the capital charge rate as a design variable. I show that under quite realistic assumptions, a higher capital charge rate than the firm's cost of capital can achieve a goal congruent solution. This result is in contrast to a statement in a recent paper that explicitly addresses the issue of cost of capital in residual income for performance evaluation. It states that the cost of capital is "clearly the riskless interest rate in a world of certainty or risk neutrality with no private pre-contract management information".[6] The optimality of higher capital charge rates in my setting is interesting, since empirical evidence shows the use of hurdle rates that are significantly higher than the cost of capital.[7] While this result has been usually explained in the context of agency models with managerial private information, my explanation is simply a consequence of the existence of the option to wait.

The remaining of the chapter is organized as follows. Section 5.2 describes the basic model of an investment opportunity with the option to wait. In section 5.3, alternative residual income based performance measures are compared. Section 5.4 extends the basic model to a setting where the investment project consists of several periods. Section 5.5 discusses the main results and section 5.6 concludes.

---

[5] Note, that I do not propose this treatment of the option for external accounting purposes. These adjustments should only serve for performance evaluation purposes, where capitalization and depreciation of the option value lies in headquarters' discretion.

[6] Christensen et al. (2002), p. 2.

[7] See Poterba & Summers (1995).

5.2 Description of the Basic Model

I consider a setting with headquarters that acts on behalf of the owners of a company, and a manager of an investment center that is a division of this company. The manager of the investment center faces an investment opportunity that can be postponed for one period. If she invests immediately, the investment opportunity is not available in the next period. If she waits, she can undertake the investment in the next period. The project consists of an initial investment outlay and cash flows from operations. To keep the model simple, I assume that all cash inflows from the project are realized in the period, which follows the period of the initial investment. This assumption will be relaxed in section 5.4. The project can be carried out either immediately or in the next period. Since the project can be postponed, it includes an option to wait. For simplicity, I assume that if the project is not carried out in the second period, the opportunity is gone forever.

If the project is carried out immediately, the firm has to pay the initial investment outlay b in $t = 0$ and receives a cash flow c_1 in $t = 1$. The net present value of the project, if carried out immediately, is therefore given by

$$V_0(c_1) = -b + c_1 \cdot \frac{1}{1+r} \tag{5.1}$$

where r is the firm's cost of capital. If the project is postponed and carried out in the subsequent period, the firm has to pay b in $t = 1$ and receives c_2 in $t = 2$. The net present value of the project in $t = 1$ is then given by

$$V_1(c_2) = -b + c_2 \cdot \frac{1}{1+r} \tag{5.2}$$

At the time, the first decision has to be made, the manager knows the value of c_1, while headquarters does not know the exact value of the first period cash flow. Both have the same expectations on the cash flows in the second period, if the project is postponed. Hence, at the time of the first decision, $\tilde{c}_2$ is a random variable for both headquarters and the manager. If the project is postponed, the manager privately gets information about the realization of $\tilde{c}_2$, while headquarters does not learn anything about the value of the second period cash flow before it is realized. Figure 5.1 summarizes the sequence of events and the decision tree.

From headquarters' perspective, the optimal investment strategy is determined by a decision tree that can be solved backwards. Suppose, the investment decision in $t = 0$ has been postponed. Then in $t = 1$,

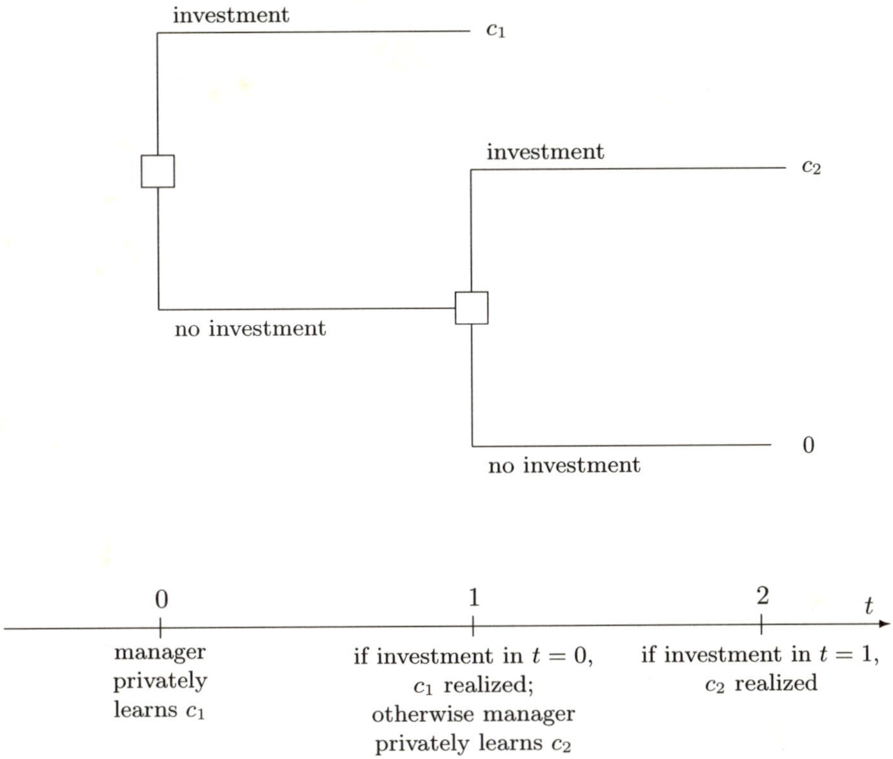

Fig. 5.1. Decision tree and sequence of events

the optimal decision is to invest, whenever the net present value V_1 is nonnegative. Therefore the value of the option to invest in $t = 1$ is given by

$$W_1 = E[\max\{V_1(\tilde{c_2}), 0\}] \tag{5.3}$$

If the investment has been carried out in $t = 0$, then there is nothing to decide on in $t = 1$, since the investment opportunity has already been realized. The optimal decision in $t = 0$ must take into account the optimal decision in $t = 1$, given a particular initial decision. It is optimal to invest, whenever the value of immediate investment is at least as high as the discounted value of the option to invest in the subsequent period. That is

$$V_0(c_1) \geq \frac{1}{1+r} \cdot W_1 \tag{5.4}$$

In general, this requirement is more demanding than the usual net present value rule since the value of W_1 might well be greater than zero, but cannot be negative. If headquarters is perfectly informed about the cash flows in $t = 0$ and $t = 1$, respectively, it can carry out the optimal investment strategy as described above.

The manager has to be given the right incentives to carry out the optimal investment strategy. These incentives come from compensation payments that are based on the realization of residual income based performance measures. The utility of the manager is determined by the discounted expected value of his compensation payments, which are assumed to be a linear function of the performance measure:

$$U(c_1) = \frac{1}{1+r_M} \cdot k \cdot RI_1(c_1) + \frac{1}{(1+r_M)^2} \cdot k \cdot E[RI_2(\tilde{c_2})] \tag{5.5}$$

In this expression, k is the linear bonus parameter, RI_1 and RI_2 are the residual income measures in period 1 and 2, respectively, and r_M is the interest rate the manager uses to discount future compensation payments. I allow this interest rate to be different from the company's cost of capital. As in the previous chapter, it is reasonable to assume that the manager's discount rate is higher than the company's, because the manager might leave the firm before all benefits of the investment have been realized or because she does not have the same access to the capital market.

5.3 Comparison of Alternative Residual Income-Based Performance Measures

5.3.1 Simple Depreciation Policy

The objective of this chapter is to compare the properties of alternative residual income based performance measures. The simplest way to calculate residual income is to fully depreciate the investment outlay during the useful life of the project and to use the company's cost of capital to determine the capital charges. A simple depreciation policy only capitalizes investment outlays and fully depreciates the investment expenditures over the useful life of the project. In my simple setting, where the useful life is one period, the whole investment outlays are depreciated in the period that follows the time of investment. If no investment takes place, there are no cash flows and, consequently, residual income is zero. If investment takes place in the second period ($t = 1$), residual income takes the form

$$RI_2(c_2) = c_2 - b - r \cdot b = c_2 - (1 + r) \cdot b \tag{5.6}$$

Similarly, if investment takes place in the first period ($t = 0$), residual income becomes

$$RI_1(c_1) = c_1 - b - r \cdot b = c_1 - (1 + r) \cdot b \tag{5.7}$$

The optimal investment strategy from the manager's perspective in the presence of a waiting option can be solved by backward induction. A manager, whose compensation is based on residual income, and whose utility is determined by the utility function (5.5) will invest in the second period, whenever her utility from investing is higher than her utility from not investing, that is

$$\frac{1}{1 + r_M} \cdot k \cdot (c_2 - (1 + r) \cdot b) \geq 0 \tag{5.8}$$

Factoring out $(1 + r)$ and substituting the expression in brackets by (5.2) yields

$$\frac{1 + r}{1 + r_M} \cdot k \cdot V_1 \geq 0 \tag{5.9}$$

Hence from the manager's perspective, it is optimal to invest in the second period, whenever the net present value of the project is positive, regardless of both the value of the bonus coefficient k and the discount rate of the manager.

Now I turn to the first period. Using utility function (5.5), it is optimal to invest in the first period, if and only if

$$\frac{1}{1 + r_M} \cdot k \cdot (c_1 - (1 + r) \cdot b) \geq \frac{1}{(1 + r_M)^2} \cdot k \cdot E[\max\{\tilde{c_2} - (1 + r) \cdot b, 0\}] \tag{5.10}$$

Factoring out $(1 + r)$ on each side, substituting by (5.1) and (5.3), respectively, and multiplying both sides by $(1 + r_M)/[(1 + r) \cdot k]$ results in

$$V_0 - \frac{1}{1 + r_M} \cdot W_1 \geq 0 \tag{5.11}$$

Comparing this relation with the optimal investment strategy from headquarters' point of view given by (5.4) shows that for the first decision, the discount rate of the manager is important. The investment decision of the manager coincides with headquarters' optimal investment decision, if and only if the manager's discount rate is the same as headquarters'. If the manager's interest rate is higher (i.e. a lower discount factor), the manager invests too early, because she discounts future benefits from the option to wait at a higher rate than headquarters. As pointed out earlier in this chapter, this case seems to be quite realistic. Since residual income in practice is often implemented in this way, one should expect that managers, whose compensation is based on residual income, do not optimally exercise their timing options and overinvest in the presence of an option to wait. If on the other hand the manager's interest rate is lower than the company's cost of capital, the manager will wait too long with investing and therefore underinvestment occurs.

5.3.2 Capitalization of the Option Value

The simple depreciation policy as described in the previous section 5.3.1 does not consider the option value, i.e. the value of waiting to invest. If, for instance, investment takes place in the first period, the option to wait is exercised and therefore looses its value. However, a performance measure based on this simple depreciation policy does not take into account this change in option value. Therefore, residual income does not fully capture the correct value of investment on a period-by-period basis. To overcome this flaw, the value of the waiting option has to be considered if investment has taken place in the first period, and subsequently depreciated according to the value creation process.

Using this idea, the option is treated as an interest bearing asset that has to be depreciated when exercised or expired. Hence, the residual income measure in the first period in the case of investment is

$$
\begin{aligned}
RI_1(c_1) &= c_1 - \left(b + \frac{1}{1+r} \cdot W_1\right) - r \cdot \left(b + \frac{1}{1+r} \cdot W_1\right) \qquad (5.12)\\
&= c_1 - (1+r) \cdot \left(b + \frac{1}{1+r} \cdot W_1\right)
\end{aligned}
$$

By accruing interest on the option value, the residual income measure in the case of no investment in the first period is zero.

Investing in the first period means that the waiting option has been exercised. Therefore there is no investment opportunity and no option value in the second period. Consequently, the residual income measure in this case is also zero. If the option has not been exercised in the first period, it can be exercised in the second period (but not later). Then residual income becomes

$$
\begin{aligned}
RI_2(c_2) &= c_2 - (b + W_1) - r \cdot (b + W_1) \qquad (5.13)\\
&= c_2 - (1+r) \cdot (b + W_1),
\end{aligned}
$$

if investment takes place and

$$RI_2(c_2) = -(1+r) \cdot W_1, \tag{5.14}$$

if no investment takes place. Hence the value of the option is depreciated in the second period, regardless if the investment is made or not.

Again, the optimal investment strategy of the manager under the so defined performance measure can be derived by backward induction. Maximizing her utility, the manager will invest in the second period, if and only if

$$\frac{1}{1+r_M} \cdot k \cdot (c_2-(1+r) \cdot (b+W_1)) \geq \frac{1}{(1+r_M)^2} \cdot k \cdot (-(1+r) \cdot W_1). \tag{5.15}$$

This expression simplifies to $V_1 \geq 0$, which is headquarters' optimal investment criterion. Hence, residual income is a goal congruent performance measure for the last decision.

In the first period, the manager will invest, if and only if her compensation payments with immediate investment are at least as high as her expected compensation payments when she waits:

$$\begin{aligned} &\frac{1}{1+r_M} \cdot k \cdot \left(c_1 - (1+r) \cdot \left(b + \frac{1}{1+r} \cdot W_1\right)\right) \geq \\ &\frac{1}{(1+r_M)^2} \cdot k \cdot E[\max\{\tilde{c_2} - (1+r) \cdot (b+W_1), -(1+r) \cdot W_1\}]. \end{aligned} \tag{5.16}$$

Simplifying and substituting by (5.1) and (5.3) yields $V_0 \geq 1/(1+r) \cdot W_1$, which is exactly headquarters' objective in the first period. Most interestingly, this result does not depend on the manager's interest rate. The reason is that the way residual income is calculated, effectively maps the value creation process completely into the performance measure. By depreciating the option value in the last period, the expected compensation payments in the last period are zero from first period's perspective. The manager knows that the option value will be depreciated in the last period if no investment occurs in the first period, no matter whether she invests or does not invest in the last period. This depreciation charge exactly offsets her expected compensation resulting from the expected cash inflows of the project in the last period. Therefore, differences in discounting future payments between headquarters and the manager do not matter. To obtain this separation, headquarters must commit to depreciate the option value even in the case, when the optimal decision in the second period is not to invest.

On the other hand, if the manager invests in the first period, the discounted cash flow from the project not only has to exceed the initial investment outlay, but also the value of the option to wait that vanishes with investment. This additional value is reflected by an additional depreciation amount that exceeds the investment outlay and again fully reflects the value creation process. Thus, the manager uses her private information about investment opportunities in a way that maximizes the value of the company.

5.3.3 Raising the Hurdle Rate

The last subsection showed that in order to obtain a goal congruent performance measure, residual income can be adjusted by capitalizing and depreciating the option value. Although the idea is quite attractive, these adjustments seem to be not very common in practice. A more prevalent adjustment is raising the capital charge rate in the residual income measure above the value that is given by the cost of capital and simultaneously maintaining the simple depreciation policy as described in section 5.3.1. This section therefore analyzes two questions. Firstly, is there a set of capital charge rates that achieves goal congruent investment incentives with the simple depreciation policy as used in section 5.3.1? In this case, the goal congruent investment policy with the adjustments in the last section can be replicated by simply adjusting the capital charge rates in the residual income measure. Secondly, in many cases it is desirable to keep the capital charge rates constant over time. Then a natural question is, if the result in section 5.3.1 can be improved by generally raising or decreasing the capital charge rate.

I start with the first question and aim on obtaining the set of optimal capital charge rates ρ_1 and ρ_2 for the first and the second period, respectively. In the last period, the simple depreciation schedule achieves goal congruence as shown in section 5.3.1 by using the capital charge rate $\rho_2 = r$. Therefore, the optimal capital charge rate for the second period is the company's cost of capital. In the first period, the critical cash flow c_1^*, below which the investment should be postponed and above which it should be carried out immediately is given by condition (5.4) and can be written in the following way:

$$-b + \frac{1}{1+r} \cdot c_1^* = \frac{1}{1+r} \cdot W_1. \tag{5.17}$$

In contrast, the manager's critical cash flow level in the first period is determined by her utility function (5.5). She will invest, when the cash flow is above the critical cash flow c_1^M, given by

$$\frac{1}{1+r_M} \cdot k \cdot (c_1^M - (1+r) \cdot b) = \frac{1}{(1+r_M)^2} \cdot k \cdot E[\max\{\tilde{c}_2 - (1+r) \cdot b, 0\}], \tag{5.18}$$

where residual income is calculated with the simple depreciation policy and using the capital charge rates ρ_1 and ρ_2. Setting $c_1^M = c_1^*$, substituting c_1^* by (5.17) and the expectation on the right-hand side by (5.3), and simplifying gives the following expression for the capital charge rate in the first period:

$$\rho_1 = r + \frac{r_M - r}{1 + r_M} \cdot \frac{W_1}{b}. \tag{5.19}$$

If headquarters applies this capital charge rate for the first period, $\rho_2 = r$ for the second period and uses a simple depreciation policy, i.e. fully depreciates the investment outlays over the useful life of the project, the manager's investment policy is goal congruent. In the case of an impatient manager ($r_M > r$), the capital charge rate in the first period is always larger than the company's cost of capital since the last term on the right-hand side in (5.19) is always positive. As mentioned in the introductory section of this chapter, this result coincides with empirically observable behavior that companies use capital charge rates that are higher than the cost of capital.[8] Most interestingly, this explanation for higher hurdle rates is different from previous theoretical work that explains this observation with asymmetric information where the manager has to be given an informational rent.[9] In my model the higher hurdle rate arises from the existence of an alternative mutually exclusive investment opportunity at a different point in time.[10] This explanation obviously challenges the hypothesis that explains higher hurdle rates with the limitation of managerial information rents.[11] Which one has more explanatory power deserves further investigation, but is beyond the scope of this work.

So far I have shown how to obtain the optimal goal congruent solution with residual income as a performance measure by adjusting the capital charge rate in each point in time. Since companies rather seem

[8] See Poterba & Summers (1995).

[9] See Antle & Eppen (1985); Bernardo et al. (2001); Baldenius (2002); Dutta & Reichelstein (2002b).

[10] The informational requirements of using a higher hurdle rate are discussed in section 5.5 below.

[11] A third hypothesis that will be not discussed here, explains higher hurdle rates with shortage of capital, which are a consequence of financing restrictions.

to use constant instead of different hurdle rates across time, an interesting question is, if a general adjustment of the capital charge rate to a constant level across time can improve the incentive properties of residual income compared to a simple depreciation policy without adjustments in the capital charge rates. A general change of the capital charge rate cannot achieve goal congruence for all decisions, because goal congruence of the last decision requires a capital charge rate that is equal to the cost of capital, whereas the capital charge rate for the first decision is generally not equal to the cost of capital. The question now is, whether constantly increasing the capital charge rate improves or worsens the investment decision.

For the following discussion suppose that the manager's discount rate is higher than the company's cost of capital. Increasing the capital charge rate for both periods above the cost of capital has two effects. In the second period the manager will generally underinvest, since the higher capital charges in the residual income measure do not comply with the net present value rule. This result follows from the assumption that the timing option has to be exercised in the second period, so there is no value in postponing the decision again. Since both decisions are interdependent, underinvestment in the second period reduces the option value and therefore has an indirect impact on the decision in the first period. A reduced value of the waiting option means that the manager will invest earlier compared to the optimal investment policy. This effect is reinforced by the fact that the manager has a higher discount rate and therefore puts less value on the timing option anyway. Hence the manager invests too early. However, in the first period the higher capital charge rate makes investment less attractive and therefore the manager will invest later. If the value of the option would not have been reduced by the indirect effect, the manager would implement the optimal exercising strategy in the first period, when the capital charge rate comes to the value given by (5.19). The indirect effect causes a deviation from this value.

From the above discussion, it becomes clear that a goal congruent solution cannot be obtained with a uniform capital charge rate and a simple depreciation policy. However, increasing the capital charge rate above the level of the cost of capital can improve a decentralized investment policy. Quantifying this improvement and calculating the exact value of the increased cost of capital requires a specification of the expectations of headquarters that is beyond the scope of this work.

5.4 Extending the Project Life to Many Periods

In order to emphasize the most important effects of different capitalization rules and capital charge rates, I kept the analysis of a timing option as simple as possible. Specifically, I assumed that all cash flows are realized in the period that follows the initial investment. A more realistic investment model has to allow for more than one period of cash inflows. Then depreciation issues, in particular the intertemporal distribution of depreciation, become important. In this section I therefore focus on a project that contains a sequence of cash inflows, and that again can be postponed by one period. For instance, think of the investment opportunity as an option to invest into a marketing campaign that can be carried out either now or next period. Here I restrict myself on showing that a similar capitalization rule like in the previous analysis leads to a goal congruent solution. It is straightforward to verify that the same reasoning as in the previous subsection applies for a hurdle rate policy.

Now the project is modelled by an initial investment outlay b and a sequence of cash flows from operations c_t where $1 \leq t \leq T$. The cash flows are assumed to be the product of a profitability parameter y_0 and a distributional parameter x_t. While the latter reflects the distribution of cash flows over time, the former can be viewed as the absolute level of profitability of the project. In the case of a marketing campaign, for example, the distributional parameter can reflect the impact of the marketing investment on the subsequent cash flows over time. In this case, it is reasonable to assume decreasing cash flows over time, since the potential impact of the marketing investment is highest directly after the campaign has been released. I further assume that this distributional parameter is common knowledge for both headquarters and the manager. However, the manager is presumed to be better informed about the absolute level of profitability of the investment. This assumption can be justified, because the manager has more knowledge about the particular market she is operating in. The net present value of the project, if carried out immediately, is therefore given by

$$V_0(y_0) = \sum_{t=1}^{T} x_t \cdot y_0 \cdot q^{-t}, \tag{5.20}$$

where $q^{-t} = (1+r)^{-t}$ is the discount factor and r is the company's cost of capital. Since the investment can be postponed, there is an alternative investment opportunity one period from now. This investment opportunity is assumed to have the same characteristics as the investment opportunity described above with one exception. From today's perspective, the profitability parameter $\tilde{y}_1$ that determines the profitability of investment, if postponed, is a random variable for both headquarters and the manager. In period 1, the manager privately learns the true value of the random variable. The net present value of the postponed project in $t = 1$ is therefore determined by

$$V_1(y_1) = \sum_{t=1}^{T} x_t \cdot y_1 \cdot q^{-t}. \tag{5.21}$$

In the second period, investment is desirable from headquarters' perspective, if $V_1(y_1) \geq 0$. In the first period, the condition for investment being profitable is $V_0(y_0) \geq q^{-1} \cdot W_1$, where again $W_1 = E[\max\{V_1(\tilde{y}_1), 0\}]$ is the value of the option to invest in the second period. The manager chooses her investment decision according to utility maximization, where her utility is given by

$$U(y_0) = \sum_{t=1}^{T} k \cdot RI_t(y_0) \cdot q_M^{-t} + E\left[\sum_{t=2}^{T+1} k \cdot RI_t(\tilde{y}_1) \cdot q_M^{-t}\right]. \tag{5.22}$$

Here, k is the bonus coefficient, $RI_t(\cdot)$ is residual income in period t, and $q_M^{-t} = (1 + r_M)^{-t}$ is the discount factor of the manager.

I now aim on showing the existence of accounting rules for the design of the residual income measure that achieve goal congruence for investment decisions with a waiting option. A natural candidate for it would be a set of rules that capitalizes the option value at the time of its emergence and depreciates the option value, when the option has been either exercised or expired, as described in section 5.3.2. Since I assumed a multi-period setting, the depreciation rules now come into place. Previous literature has shown that the relative benefit depreciation schedule has desirable incentive properties.[12] According to this suggestion, the depreciation charges in each period are calculated in a way, that the sum of depreciation and capital charges in each period denoted $z_t \cdot b$ matches the value of the time-weighted cash inflows from the project, where $z_t \cdot b$ is defined according to

$$z_t \cdot b = d_t \cdot b + r \cdot B_{t-1}. \tag{5.23}$$

In this expression, $\{d_t\}_{t=1+i}^{T+i}$ is the depreciation schedule, with $i = 0$, if investment occurs in the first period, $i = 1$, if investment occurs in the second period, and $\sum_{t=1+i}^{T+i} d_t = 1$, $i \in \{0, 1\}$. The depreciation schedule

[12] See Rogerson (1997); Reichelstein (1997).

determines the asset value B_{t-1} according to $B_t = B_{t-1} - d_t \cdot b$ with $B_0 = b$. Thus, the periodic charges can be rewritten as

$$z_t \cdot b = d_t \cdot b + r \cdot b \cdot \left(1 - \sum_{j=1+i}^{t-1+i} d_j \right). \tag{5.24}$$

The relative benefit depreciation schedule proposes to choose the periodic charges according to

$$z_t = \frac{x_t}{\sum_{j=1+i}^{T+i} x_j \cdot q^{-j-i}}. \tag{5.25}$$

Note that the $T+1$ equations given by (5.24) and (5.25) uniquely determine the depreciation schedule $\{d_t\}_{t=1+i}^{T+i}$. This schedule together with the accounting rules described in section 5.3.2 specify the residual income measure. Suppose that the manager has not invested in the first period. Using this measure, in the second period the manager decides to invest, if and only if her utility from investing exceeds her utility from not investing:

$$\sum_{t=2}^{T+1} k \cdot (x_t \cdot y_1 - z_t \cdot (b + W_1)) \cdot q_M^{-t-1} \geq \sum_{t=2}^{T+1} k \cdot (-z_t \cdot W_1) \cdot q_M^{-t-1}, \tag{5.26}$$

where W_1 again is the value of the timing option defined by $W_1 = E[\max\{V_1(\tilde{y}_1), 0\}]$. Note that the amount to be depreciated is the sum of investment outlays and the option value of the waiting option from the first period. Substituting (5.25), factoring out $x_t / \left(\sum_{j=1+i}^{T+i} x_j \cdot q^{-j-i} \right)$ on either side, dividing by k and simplifying yields

$$\left(\sum_{t=2}^{T+1} x_t \cdot y_1 \cdot q_M^{-t-1} - b \right) \cdot \left(\sum_{t=2}^{T+1} \left[\frac{x_t}{\sum_{j=1+i}^{T+i} x_j \cdot q^{-j-i}} \cdot q_M^{-t-1} \right] \right) \geq 0. \tag{5.27}$$

This expression yields headquarters' condition for the optimal decision in the second period. Hence goal congruence is achieved for the decision in the second period. Now turn to the first period. Residual income is calculated according to the following rule. If the manager invests, the sum of the investment outlay and the discounted value of the waiting option will be depreciated according to the relative benefit depreciation schedule. If she does not invest, residual income will be zero. Hence, her decision is to invest, if and only if

$$\sum_{t=1}^{T} k \cdot (x_t \cdot y_0 - z_t \cdot (b + q^{-1} \cdot W_1)) \cdot q_M^{-t} \geq \qquad (5.28)$$
$$E[\max\{\sum_{t=2}^{T+1} k \cdot (x_t \cdot y_1 - z_t \cdot (b + W_1)) \cdot q_M^{-t},$$
$$\sum_{t=2}^{T+1} k \cdot (-z_t \cdot W_1) \cdot q_M^{-t}\}].$$

As in the case with one cash inflow, the value of the expectation and therefore the right-hand side of this condition is 0. This can be seen by subtracting $\sum_{t=2}^{T+1} k \cdot (-z_t \cdot W_1) \cdot q_M^{-t}$ from each argument in the maximum-function on the right-hand side of the above inequality (5.28). Again, the reason is that the value of the waiting option is depreciated regardless whether investment occurs in the second period while the benefits only realize with a certain probability. Using (5.25), factoring out $x_t / \left(\sum_{j=1}^{T} x_j \cdot q^{-j}\right)$ and simplifying yields

$$\sum_{t=1}^{T} (V_0(y_0) - q^{-1} \cdot W_1) \cdot \frac{x_t}{\sum_{j=1}^{T} x_j \cdot q^{-j}} \geq 0, \qquad (5.29)$$

which again results in headquarters' objective for first period investment. Hence the main result of the analysis, the existence of a goal congruent residual income based performance measure when there is a timing option, carries over to the case of multi period investments.

5.5 Advantages and Disadvantages of the Proposed Design Alternatives

The analysis of the model shows two alternative ways to achieve a goal congruent residual income measure in the presence of a timing option. The first, capitalizing the option value and depreciating it when an investment decision is made or uncertainty resolves, has the important advantage that it can be applied even if headquarters does not know anything about the manager's discount rate. The only informational requirement for headquarters is to have an estimation of the option value. At the same time, headquarters does not need to know the exact value of the investment cash flows. By using residual income as a performance measure, it can use the manager's informational advantage. On the other hand, there is also a disadvantage of this kind of performance measure design. If uncertainty resolves in a bad state of nature in the second period, then no investment occurs, and the expected compensation ex ante results in a negative realized compensation ex post. Since the manager learns the realized value of cash flow before investing, she might have an incentive to leave the company. A firm concerned about retaining the manager must consider this possibility in designing the performance measure.

The second way for designing residual income avoids this shortcoming. By using the capital charge rate, the hurdle for the first decision is increased without affecting the performance measure in the second period. Therefore, even a bad realization of the uncertain state variable does not change the manager's incentives to stay in the firm. She simply can react by not choosing to invest in the second period. However, the informational requirements for headquarters are much more demanding than in the previous alternative. Headquarters not only must have an estimation of the option value. It also must know the manager's discount rate, as shown by equation (5.19).

The above discussion suggests conditions for choosing the first or second alternative. In situations, where managers have specific knowledge that is important for the company, retention of the manager is an important issue. In this case, raising the hurdle rate is the more attractive adjustment in the residual income measure and the company should put much effort in determining the manager's discount rate in order to correctly determine the capital charge rate. If the manager can be easily replaced, the retention objective is not so important. Then the first alternative is the better one, since its informational requirements are less demanding.

An additional issue that has been neglected so far is the possible manipulation of the option value by the manager. Both alternatives only work in situations, where headquarters and the manager have symmetric valuations of the option value. If the manager is better informed not only about the cash flows but also the option value, additional difficulties arise. Then headquarters is neither able to determine the capitalization value, nor the adjusted capital charge rate, and goal congruence cannot be assured. In this case, the accounting system is not able to provide a performance measures that achieves a goal congruent solution for the investment problem and alternative performance measures like for instance the stock price should be considered.

5.6 Implications for Corporate Practice and Further Research

This chapter contributes to both the literature on real options valuation, and the literature on controlling investment decisions. For the former, the analysis uses the widely neglected fact that investment decisions are often made decentrally. The analysis shows one possibility to deal with this delegated decision making in a real options framework by using an accounting based performance measure. The contribution for the latter is that the analysis describes a way to obtain goal congruent performance measures when the arrival of new information has an influence on investment behavior. The use of residual income in such situations seems to be promising, but this metric has to be carefully designed and adjusted, taking into account the distribution of information between headquarters and the divisional manager.

An empirical implication of the analysis in this chapter is that for companies which use a residual income based reward system, the capital charge rate should be higher, if there are valuable waiting options. This should be true particularly for industries, where investments can be relatively easily postponed without giving competitors the opportunity to undertake the investment themselves. It would be interesting to test this hypothesis against competing hypothesis that explain higher hurdle rates by managerial private information.

Further theoretical research can extend this chapter's results in different directions. First, this analysis assumes that the option to wait expires after the second period. With respect to the hurdle rate, the analysis of a waiting option with a longer expiration time could generalize the propositions of this chapter. In particular, uniformly increasing the hurdle rate might well be a goal congruent solution, if the option to wait has an infinite expiration time. Second, it would be interesting to further analyze the incentive properties of residual income for different types of real options like for example the option to abandon a project. Third, the results could be extended to an optimal contract setting where a manager has to provide personally costly effort to optimize the project's cash flows.

6

Implications and Conclusions

6.1 Contribution to the Literature

In this section, I will discuss this work's contribution to the literature with respect to its substance and its methodological insights. Most importantly, this work considerably extends the theoretical accounting and financial economics literature on investment incentives by significantly relaxing one of its major assumptions. This assumption restricts the set of possible investments to those, which consist of a deterministic or stochastic set of cash flows and only one - the initial - investment decision. As has been illustrated in this work with some examples, this restriction clearly is a oversimplification of many practical investment problems, since adapting investment projects to new information and making new decisions on existing projects is a major task of a company's management. And indeed, many of the recommendations of the literature on investment incentives have to be qualified or at least complemented in the light of my results.

For instance, the analysis of capital budgeting for investments that have the form of a growth option demonstrated the optimality of a staged budgeting procedure that uses the arrival of new information for budgeting decisions on parts of budgets. This phenomenon can be widely observed in the context of R&D-funding, but up to now, a theoretical explanation for it was lacking. In my model in chapter 3, headquarters uses a revelation mechanism to learn the true cost of the single stages of the R&D investment and provides funding according to this information. Like in the one-period models, capital rationing occurs. As a new aspect of my model, the extent of capital rationing strongly depends on the question whether the divisional manager has some kind of own resources, possibly from additional projects, with which she can support investment in growth options.

Recommendations by theorists as well as practitioners on the use of residual income as a managerial performance measure also have to be qualified in the presence of real options. More or less simple depreciation schedules for residual income generally do not achieve goal congruence when investment projects have some real option features. The reason is that a depreciation schedule alone is not able to capture the value of a real option, which is available immediately but has to be exercised so as to maximize the complete value of the investment project. Moreover even the direction of the distortion is not immediately clear. Depending on the type of real options associated with an investment project, overinvestment as well as underinvestment can occur. Instead of using a simple depreciation policy, the correct value of the real option has to be recognized immediately by capitalizing and subsequently depreciating it. While for external purposes this recommendations may pose serious problems due to the danger of manipulation, this adaption of residual income is shown to be optimal for performance evaluation purposes. The more general point that can be made here is that headquarters should put all available information into the performance measure. While depreciation schedules may reflect knowledge about the useful life of a project and the distribution of cash inflows, capitalization rules can be used to incorporate knowledge about valuable real options.

Besides the literature on decentral investment decision-making and investment incentives, my work complements the valuation literature on real options by analyzing the effects of incentive issues on the valuation problem. As is demonstrated in chapter 3, the valuation of a growth option significantly changes, when incentive issues are present. Due to the necessity of paying the divisional manager an informational rent in the second stage, the cost threshold, up to which investment is profitable, decreases compared to a single-person decision context. The same issue continues to hold also for the first stage. Therefore, investment in the growth option becomes less likely, which qualifies recommendations in the real options literature according to which the absolute level of investment should be strongly enlarged in the presence of growth options. Chapters 4 and 5 raise issues of implementing real option valuation in decentralized companies. It is shown that a standard application of so-called value-based management systems like Economic Value Added does not achieve a value-maximizing exercise of real options, since a divisional manager has preferences different from those of headquarters. The analysis shows that implementation issues must not be neglected in real option valuation, a statement that has been emphasized but not formally analyzed by various authors in this line of literature.[1]

From a pure methodological point of view, chapter 3 analyzes a two-period adverse selection problem. General models of this type are hard to analyze and the literature in this area is not too exhaustive.[2] My modelling differs from the existing literature that it contains a strong relationship between both periods. Investment in the second period is only feasible, if first-period investment has been undertaken. This relationship requires some adjustments in the solution procedure that have not been emphasized so far.[3] This work also demonstrates the technical simplification that can be achieved by using goal congruence models (chapters 4 and 5) compared to adverse-selection models (chapter 3) in a multi-period framework. For the former, it is not necessary to confine the form of the probability distribution. Since contractual costs are neglected, the optimization problem of headquarters reduces to a relatively simple form. Using these types of models allows conclusions on the optimal design of performance measures that go far beyond conclusions which dynamic principal-agent models would allow.

6.2 Limitations of the Analysis

The analysis in this work relies on several simplifying assumptions that are emphasized in the following discussion. Strengths and weaknesses of principal-agent models are discussed controversial in the literature. While some authors criticize the complexity of the optimal contracts[4] that cannot be found in reality, others emphasize the usefulness of principal-agent models as a framework for "highlighting problems which arise and must be considered in applying managerial accounting procedures to real-world situations."[5] Indeed, the model particularly in chapter 3 is not designed to give recommendations that are immediately transferable to corporate practice. Rather, it sheds some light on capital budgeting problems that arise in the context of growth options.

[1] See, e.g., Amram & Kulatilaka (1999), pp. 210-211.

[2] Two-period adverse selection models include Laffont & Tirole (1988); Trauzettel (1999); Courty & Li (2000). For applications in capital budgeting see Antle & Fellingham (1990); Fellingham & Young (1990).

[3] Even the model by Antle et al. (2000) which is closest to my work with respect to the methodology does not require these adjustments, because the waiting option has some properties that considerably simplify the analysis compared to a two-stage investment.

[4] See, e.g., Arrow (1985), p. 48.

[5] Baiman (1990), p. 345.

The analysis also does not include intrinsic motivation as a potential source of motivation.[6] However, in my view a separated analysis is justified by the significance of extrinsic motivation.

While the notion of growth option is fairly general, switching options and waiting options require a more specific modelling. The analysis in chapters 4 and 5 clearly relies on the particularities of this modelling. The specific modelling is necessary to keep the valuation problem simple enough to focus on incentive issues. A more general approach would clearly fail to demonstrate the effects of using different forms of residual income as a performance measure in these specific situations. Furthermore, the general idea of improving the residual income measure by considering the real option value carries over to different applications, so that focusing the analysis on specific situations seems to be justified. Indeed, the results in chapters 4 and 5 obtained for different types of real options partly go into opposite directions.

Other limitations of the analysis are its restriction to residual income as a performance measure and linear contracts. Of course, one could think of starting with a very general set of performance measures and deriving properties, an optimal performance measure must have. However, given the prevalent use of residual income in corporate practice and given the theoretical work proving the optimality of residual income as a performance measure under certain conditions compared to alternative measures of performance, the restriction on the analysis of residual income seems to be a reasonable modelling choice. The restriction on linear contracts also does not loose to much generality, since the focus of my analysis is not on the optimal choice of the bonus coefficient but on the performance measure. The analysis is likely to carry over to other forms of compensation functions, as long as they are increasing in the performance measure over the whole range of possible outcomes.

6.3 Empirical Implications

Although all models in this work strongly simplify reality to gain insights on the structure and interaction of incentive effects and real options, the propositions of these models may serve as a starting point for the development of hypotheses that can be verified empirically. The analysis in chapter 3 yields new and testable implications for investments that have the form of growth options. First of all, in terms of the

[6] See Davila (2003), p. 1398. for the relationship of intrinsic motivation and external rewards in the context of R&D.

capital budgeting procedure, the model predicts a staged funding of projects where the arrival of new information is important. Therefore, one should observe a staged budgeting procedure more frequently for projects with this feature than for other types of investment projects. For example, when the firm has high R&D expenditures, the probability of observing a staged budgeting procedure should be higher. Another interesting implication results from the fact that the severity of the underinvestment problem depends on the participation constraints. Linking these to organizational design, I predict that the underinvestment problem is more severe, when the manager is responsible only for one project than if she has responsibility for different projects and the ability to shift funds between projects. In the latter case, the hurdle rates should be lower than in the former case.

Turning to the analysis of residual income as a performance measure in the context of switching options, the model predicts that a standard application of residual income as a performance measure should result in underinvestment for projects with switching options or growth options. It would be interesting to compare investment activities that have real option features with those that are simple investment projects in firms using residual income as a performance measure. Another interesting question is, whether this underinvestment problem for real option projects is lower in firms that do not use residual income based performance measures.

While I predict underinvestment for switching options and growth options, the use of residual income as a performance measure has a different effect for investments that can be postponed. When there is a valuable waiting option, a standard use of residual income without adjustments results in some kind of overinvestment: the manager invests too early. This prediction is consistent with anecdotal evidence on the effects of using residual income for performance evaluation purposes, which states that the use of residual income strongly encourages a higher level of investment activities. My analysis proposes that this level may be even too high. With regard to investment hurdle rates, the analysis shows a different reason for the use of higher hurdle rates than required by standard finance theory. While in chapter 3, the need for paying the manager an information rent results in higher hurdle rates, in chapter 5 the existence of the waiting option is the reason. The model predicts that hurdle rates are higher in firms that have valuable waiting options than in firms which have not. Given that waiting options loose their value, when competition is strong,[7] I predict higher hurdle rates in less

[7] See Friedl (2000), pp. 98-119; Grenadier (1996).

competitive industries and in industries where investment opportunities can be protected by patents or other forms of property rights.

6.4 Extensions and Further Theoretical Research

There are many interesting paths for further theoretical research. I have restricted attention to investments with growth, switching, and waiting options. They cover a broad spectrum of possible applications but there are of course further real options like for example the option to mothball operations or the abandonment option.[8] Their analysis can further improve our understanding of investment incentive issues in the presence of real options. I also have only considered situations, when there is only one division and one project. If there are many projects with embedded real options, risk management issues arise. Headquarters may have an interest to optimize the whole portfolio of investments such that the risk associated with different real options can be reduced. This may lead to another choice of investment projects than which is optimal from a single divisional manager's perspective. Finally, I have restricted the analysis to a specific accounting-based performance measure. Many large companies rely on market-based performance measures, like for example stock or stock options, not only for top management but also for the divisional level. Although there are many factors that influence the market value of a company besides a divisional manager's actions, market-based performance measures are at least in principle able to capture some long-term benefits on investment activities that are difficult to be captured by accounting-based performance measures. It would thus be very interesting to explicitly allow for the use of market-based performance measures in particular for real option investments and model these additional aspects of stock-based compensation.[9] A clearer understanding of the use of these measures will allow us to improve our understanding of investment decision-making within firms.

---

[8] See, e.g., Friedl (2002b).

[9] See Dutta & Reichelstein (2000) for a model analyzing these two classes of performance measure in the context of simple investment decisions without real options.

A

Appendix

Proofs for Chapter 3

Proof of Proposition 3.1

The proof of this proposition follows the arguments in *Antle et al.* (2000). I start with the following lemma A.1.

Lemma A.1. *There is a single investment cost target in t_1, denoted I_1^T. In t_2, there is an investment cost target function, denoted $I_2^T(I_1)$, which depends on the cost report in t_1. Below each of these targets, investment takes place and above not.*

Proof of Lemma A.1

I start with the second period t_2 and the case when $d_1(I_1) = 1$. It is to prove that if investment takes place for a cost I_2 then the same investment decision will also be made, if the cost is $\hat{I}_2 < I_2$. To prove this assume the opposite. $\exists I_1, I_2, \hat{I}_2$ with $\hat{I}_2 < I_2$ and $d_2(I_1, \hat{I}_2) = 0$ while $d_2(I_1, I_2) = 1$. Then the incentive constraint (3.5) that ensures I_2 will be reported instead of $\hat{I}_2$ when the true investment cost is I_2 gives $S_2(I_1, I_2) \geq S_2(I_1, \hat{I}_2)$. In contrast, the incentive constraint (3.5) that ensures $\hat{I}_2$ will be reported instead of I_2 when the true investment cost is $\hat{I}_2$ provides $S_2(I_1, \hat{I}_2) \geq S_2(I_1, I_2) + (I_2 - \hat{I}_2)$ These two results and using that $I_2 > \hat{I}_2$ results in

$$S_2(I_1, I_2) \geq S_2(I_1, \hat{I}_2) \geq S_2(I_1, I_2) + (I_2 - \hat{I}_2) > S_2(I_1, I_2) \qquad \text{(A.1)}$$

which is a contradiction.

The proof that there is a single investment cost target also in the first period follows the same arguments and is omitted here. □

The existence of investment cost targets allows to rewrite the headquarterst́ objective function in the following way:

$$
\begin{aligned}
\max_{\{S_1(\cdot),S_2(\cdot,\cdot),d_1(\cdot),d_2(\cdot,\cdot)\}} & \int_{\underline{I}_1}^{I_1^T} [-S_1(I_1) - d_1(I_1)\, I_1]\, f(I_1)\, dI_1 \qquad (A.2)\\
&+ \int_{I_1^T}^{\overline{I}_1} [-S_1(I_1) - d_1(I_1)\, I_1]\, f(I_1)\, dI_1\\
&+ q \int_{\underline{I}_1}^{I_1^T} \left(\int_{\underline{I}_2}^{I_2^T(I_1)} [-S_2(I_1, I_2) + d_2(I_1, I_2)\, (V - I_2)]\, g(I_2)\, dI_2 \right)\\
&\cdot f(I_1)\, dI_1\\
&+ q \int_{\underline{I}_1}^{I_1^T} \left(\int_{I_2^T(I_1)}^{\overline{I}_2} [-S_2(I_1, I_2) + d_2(I_1, I_2)\, (V - I_2)]\, g(I_2)\, dI_2 \right) f(I_1)\, dI_1\\
&+ q \int_{I_1^T}^{\overline{I}_1} \left(\int_{\underline{I}_2}^{\overline{I}_2} [-S_2(I_1, I_2) + d_2(I_1, I_2)\, (V - I_2)]\, g(I_2)\, dI_2 \right) f(I_1)\, dI_1.
\end{aligned}
$$

Substituting the decision functions with their respective values yields:

$$
\begin{aligned}
\max_{\{S_1(\cdot),S_2(\cdot,\cdot)\}} & \int_{\underline{I}_1}^{I_1^T} [-S_1(I_1) - I_1]\, f(I_1)\, dI_1 \qquad (A.3)\\
&+ \int_{I_1^T}^{\overline{I}_1} -S_1(I_1)\, f(I_1)\, dI_1\\
&+ q \int_{\underline{I}_1}^{I_1^T} \left(\int_{\underline{I}_2}^{I_2^T(I_1)} [-S_2(I_1, I_2) + (V - I_2)]\, g(I_2)\, dI_2 \right)\\
&\cdot f(I_1)\, dI_1\\
&+ q \int_{\underline{I}_1}^{I_1^T} \left(\int_{I_2^T(I_1)}^{\overline{I}_2} -S_2(I_1, I_2)\, g(I_2)\, dI_2 \right) f(I_1)\, dI_1\\
&+ q \int_{I_1^T}^{\overline{I}_1} \left(\int_{\underline{I}_2}^{\overline{I}_2} -S_2(I_1, I_2)\, g(I_2)\, dI_2 \right) f(I_1)\, dI_1
\end{aligned}
$$

I proceed by using the incentive constraints (3.5) and (3.6) to derive some properties of the slack functions $S_1(I_1)$ and $S_2(I_1, I_2)$. Distinguishing three cases at $t = 2$ and two cases at $t = 1$ yields:

- $t = 2$: $I_1 \leq I_1^T \wedge I_2, \hat{I}_2 \leq I_2^T(I_1)$
  The incentive constraints (3.5) at $t = 2$ imply

$$S_2(I_1, I_2) \geq S_2(I_1, \hat{I}_2) + (\hat{I}_2 - I_2)$$

and

$$S_2(I_1, \hat{I}_2) \geq S_2(I_1, I_2) + (I_2 - \hat{I}_2).$$

Rearranging these two weak inequalities shows that

$$S_2(I_1, I_2) - S_2(I_1, \hat{I}_2) = (\hat{I}_2 - I_2).$$

Because this equation must hold for any $I_2, \hat{I}_2 \leq I_2^T(I_1)$, it must also hold for $I_2, I_2^T(I_1)$. Therefore, the slack function takes the form

$$S_2(I_1, I_2) = \alpha(I_1) + (I_2^T(I_1) - I_2) \; \forall I_1 \leq I_1^T \wedge I_2 \leq I_2^T(I_1) \quad \text{(A.4)}$$

with $\alpha(\cdot)$ being an arbitrary function of I_1.

- $t = 2$: $I_1 \leq I_1^T \wedge I_2 > I_2^T(I_1)$
  Using the above result, the incentive constraints (3.5) at $t = 2$ for I_2 and $I_2^T(I_1)$ imply

  $$S_2(I_1, I_2) \geq \alpha(I_1) + (I_2^T(I_1) - I_2)$$

  and

  $$\alpha(I_1) \geq S_2(I_1, I_2).$$

  Rearranging these two weak inequalities implies

  $$\alpha(I_1) \geq S_2(I_1, I_2) \geq \alpha(I_1) + (I_2^T(I_1) - I_2).$$

  Taking the limit $I_2 \longrightarrow I_2^T(I_1)$ yields

  $$S_2(I_1, I_2) = \alpha(I_1) \; \forall I_1 \leq I_1^T \wedge I_2 > I_2^T(I_1). \quad \text{(A.5)}$$

- $t = 2$: $I_1 > I_1^T$
  If $I_1 > I_1^T$, then $d_2(I_1, I_2) = 0$. From the incentive constraints, it can be shown in a similar way that

  $$S_2(I_1, I_2) = \beta(I_1) \; \forall I_1 > I_1^T, I_2. \quad \text{(A.6)}$$

- $t = 1$: $I_1, \hat{I}_1 \leq I_1^T$
  The incentive constraints (3.6) for two investment costs $I_1, \hat{I}_1 \leq I_1^T$ yield

  $$S_1(I_1) + q\,E[S_2(I_1, I_2)] \geq S_1(\hat{I}_1) + (\hat{I}_1 - I_1) + q\,E[S_2(\hat{I}_1, I_2)]$$

  and

  $$S_1(\hat{I}_1) + q\,E[S_2(\hat{I}_1, I_2)] \geq S_1(I_1) + (I_1 - \hat{I}_1) + q\,E[S_2(I_1, I_2)]$$

  with

  $$E[S_2(\cdot, I_2)] = \alpha(\cdot) + \int_{\underline{I}_2}^{I_2^T(\cdot)} (I_2^T(\cdot) - I_2)\, g(I_2)\, dI_2.$$

Bringing these weak inequalities together yields

$$S_1(I_1) + q\,E[S_2(I_1, I_2)] = S_1(\hat{I}_1) + q\,E[S_2(\hat{I}_1, I_2)] + (\hat{I}_1 - I_1).$$

Because this equation must hold for arbitrary $I_1, \hat{I}_1 \leq I_1^T$, it must also hold for $\hat{I}_1 = I_1^T$. Therefore,

$$S_1(I_1) + q\,E[S_2(I_1, I_2)] = \gamma + (I_1^T - I_1)\ \forall I_1 \leq I_1^T \tag{A.7}$$

with γ being a constant.

- $t = 1$: $I_1 > I_1^T$
  Using the above result, the incentive constraints (3.6) at $t = 1$ for I_1 and I_1^T imply

$$S_1(I_1) + q\,\beta(I_1) \geq \gamma + (I_1^T - I_1)$$

and

$$\gamma \geq S_1(I_1) + q\,\beta(I_1).$$

Rearranging these two weak inequalities implies

$$\gamma \geq S_1(I_1) + q\,\beta(I_1) \geq \gamma + (I_1^T - I_1).$$

Taking the limit $I_1 \longrightarrow I_1^T$ yields

$$\gamma = S_1(I_1) + q\,\beta(I_1)\ \forall I_1 > I_1^T \tag{A.8}$$

With these properties, the objective function can be simplified to

$$\begin{aligned}
&\int_{\underline{I}_1}^{I_1^T} [-\gamma - I_1^T + q\,E[S_2(I_1, I_2)]]\, f(I_1)\, dI_1 \qquad\qquad (A.9)\\
&+ q \int_{\underline{I}_1}^{I_1^T} \Big([-\alpha(I_1) - I_2^T(I_1) + V]G(I_2^T(I_1))\Big)\, f(I_1)\, dI_1\\
&+ q \int_{\underline{I}_1}^{I_1^T} \Big([-\alpha(I_1)][1 - G(I_2^T(I_1)]\Big)\, f(I_1)\, dI_1\\
&+ \int_{I_1^T}^{\overline{I}_1} (-\gamma)\, f(I_1)\, dI_1.
\end{aligned}$$

Now consider the participation constraints (3.2) and (3.3). From them and equations (A.4), (A.5), and (A.6), I can conclude that $\alpha(I_1) \geq 0$ and $\beta(I_1) \geq 0$. From headquarters point of view and considering the participation constraints (3.2) as well as condition (A.7), it is optimal to set $\gamma = q\,E[S_2(I_1, I_2)]$. Now consider the slack function $S_2(I_1, I_2)$. Suppose, $\alpha(I_1) = 0$. Then, the incentive constraints at $t = 1$

only hold, if $I_2^T(I_1)$ is a constant with respect to I_1, denoted I_2^T. To verify if this is optimal, consider an increase of $\alpha(I_1)$ for a given I_1. Simultaneously, $I_2^T(I_1)$ must decrease by the same amount to maintain incentives to tell the truth in $t = 1$. But reducing $I_2^T(I_1)$ is not in the interest of headquarters, because it reduces the probability of (valuable) investment in the second period. Therefore, setting $I_2^T(I_1) = I_2^T$ and $\alpha(I_1) = 0$ is optimal. Moreover, $\beta(I_1)$ and $S_1(I_1)\,\forall I_1 > I_1^T$ are determined by equation (A.8) and (3.2). Clearly, setting $\beta(I_1) = 0$ and $S_1(I_1) = E[S_2(I_1, I_2)]\,\forall I_1 > I_1^T$ is optimal from headquarters point of view. These results imply that the objective function can be written in the following way:

$$
\begin{aligned}
&F(I_1^T)(-I_1^T) \\
&+q\,G(I_2^T)F(I_1^T)(-I_2^T + V) - q\,(1 - F(I_1^T)) \int_{\underline{I}_2}^{I_2{}^T} (I_2{}^T - I_2)\, g(I_2)\, dI_2
\end{aligned}
$$

Setting $I_1^T = I_1^*$ and $I_2^T = I_2^*$ leads to the optimal decision and slack functions given in the proposition. □

Proof of Proposition 3.2

Headquarters' objective is given by

$$
\begin{aligned}
&\max_{\{I_1^T, I_2^T\}} \; U(I_1^T, I_2^T) = \\
&\max_{\{I_1^T, I_2^T\}} \; F(I_1^T)(-I_1^T) + q\,F(I_1^T)G(I_2^T)(V - I_2^T) \\
&\qquad -q\,(1 - F(I_1^T)) \int_{\underline{I}_2}^{I_2{}^T} (I_2{}^T - I_2)\, g(I_2)\, dI_2.
\end{aligned}
$$

The two first order conditions are

$$
f(I_1^*)(-I_1^*) - F(I_1^*) + q\,f(I_1^*) \int_{\underline{I}_2}^{I_2{}^*} (V - I_2)\, g(I_2)\, dI_2 = 0 \qquad \text{(A.10)}
$$

and

$$
q\,F(I_1^*)g(I_2^*)(V - I_2^*) + q\,F(I_1^*)G(I_2^*)(-1) - q\,(1 - F(I_1^*))\,G(I_2^*) = 0. \qquad \text{(A.11)}
$$

Rearranging yields

$$
I_1^* = q \int_{\underline{I}_2}^{I_2{}^*} (I_2{}^* - I_2)\, g(I_2)\, dI_2 - \frac{F(I_1^*)}{f(I_1^*)}, \qquad \text{(A.12)}
$$

$$
I_2^* = V - \frac{G(I_2^*)}{g(I_2^*)} \cdot \frac{1}{F(I_1^*)}. \qquad \text{(A.13)}
$$

For this solution to be optimal, the second order conditions have to be checked:

$$\frac{\partial^2 U}{\partial I_1^T \partial I_1^T} = -2f(I_1^T) - f'(I_1^T)\left(I_1^T - q\int_{\underline{I}_2}^{I_2{}^T} (V - I_2)\, g(I_2)\, dI_2\right)$$
$$\frac{\partial^2 U}{\partial I_2^T \partial I_2^T} = q\,[g'(I_2^T)F(I_1^T)(V - I_2^T) - g(I_2^T)F(I_1^T) - g(I_2^T)]$$
$$\frac{\partial^2 U}{\partial I_1^T \partial I_2^T} = \frac{\partial^2 U}{\partial I_2^T \partial I_1^T} = q\, f(I_1^T)g(I_2^T)(V - I_2^T).$$

For the second order conditions to hold, the Hessian matrix must be negative semi-definite around the solution determined by the first order conditions. That requires $\frac{\partial^2 U}{\partial I_1^T \partial I_1^T} \leq 0$ and $\frac{\partial^2 U}{\partial I_1^T \partial I_1^T} \cdot \frac{\partial^2 U}{\partial I_2^T \partial I_2^T} - (\frac{\partial^2 U}{\partial I_1^T \partial I_2^T})^2 \geq 0$. At the solutions I_1^* and I_2^*, given by (A.10) and (A.11), $\frac{\partial^2 U}{\partial I_1^T \partial I_1^T} = -2f(I_1^*) + f'(I_1^*)(F(I_1^*)/f(I_1^*)) < 0$. The inequality follows after some calculations from the assumption of an increasing inverse hazard rate. The determinant of the Hessian matrix is given by

$$q(-f(I_1^*) - f(I_1^*)H_1'(I_1^*))(-g(I_2^*)F(I_1^*) - g(I_2^*)H_2'(I_2^*)) - \left(q\frac{f(I_1^*)G(I_2^*)}{F(I_1^*)}\right)^2 \tag{A.14}$$

Using that the inverse hazard rates are increasing, the last expression is greater than

$$q\, f(I_1^*)\, g(I_2^*)F(I_1^*) - \left(q\frac{f(I_1^*)G(I_2^*)}{F(I_1^*)}\right)^2, \tag{A.15}$$

which simplifies to the condition given in proposition 2. The second order conditions are satisfied, if this expression is greater than 0. □

Proof of Proposition 3.3

Up to equation (A.8), the proof is the same as that of proposition 1. In contrast to that proof, the new and different participation constraints (3.16) only require the sum of the first and second period slack being nonnegative. Therefore, a negative first period slack can be compensated by an equal but positive second period slack. As above, the simplified objective function is

$$\int_{\underline{I}_1}^{I_1^T} [-\gamma - I_1^T + q\, E[S_2(I_1, I_2)]]\, f(I_1)\, dI_1 \tag{A.16}$$

$$+\, q \int_{\underline{I}_1}^{I_1^T} \left([-\alpha(I_1) - I_2^T(I_1) + V] G(I_2^T(I_1)) \right) f(I_1)\, dI_1$$

$$+\, q \int_{\underline{I}_1}^{I_1^T} \left([-\alpha(I_1)][1 - G(I_2^T(I_1))] \right) f(I_1)\, dI_1$$

$$+ \int_{I_1^T}^{\overline{I}_1} (-\gamma)\, f(I_1)\, dI_1.$$

Now it is clearly optimal for headquarters to set $\gamma = S_1(I_1) = \beta(I_1) = 0\, \forall I_1 > I_1^T$. Using the same arguments as in the proof of proposition 1, it can be shown that setting $I_2^T(I_1) = I_2^T$ and $\alpha(I_1) = 0$ is optimal. Then the objective function can be written in the following way:

$$F(I_1^T) \left(-I_1^T + q \int_{\underline{I}_2}^{I_2^T} (I_2^T - I_2)\, g(I_2)\, dI_2 \right) \qquad \text{(A.17)}$$
$$+ q\, G(I_2^T) F(I_1^T)(-I_2^T + V)$$

For $I_1^T = I_1^{PC}$ and $I_2^T = I_2^{PC}$, these results imply the optimal decision and slack functions given in the proposition. □

Proof of Proposition 3.4

Now, headquarters' objective is given by

$$\max_{\{I_1^T, I_2^T\}} \; U^{PC}(I_1^T, I_2^T) =$$
$$\max_{\{I_1^T, I_2^T\}} \; F(I_1^T)(-I_1^T) + q\, F(I_1^T) G(I_2^T)(V - I_2^T)$$
$$-q\,(1 - F(I_1^T)) \int_{\underline{I}_2}^{I_2{}^T} (I_2{}^T - I_2)\, g(I_2)\, dI_2.$$

The two first order conditions are

$$f(I_1^{PC})(-I_1^{PC} \qquad \text{(A.18)}$$
$$+ q \int_{\underline{I}_2}^{I_2{}^{PC}} (I_2{}^{PC} - I_2)\, g(I_2)\, dI_2) - F(I_1^{PC})$$
$$+ q\, f(I_1^{PC}) G(I_2^{PC})(V - I_2^{PC}) = 0$$

and

$$q\, F(I_1^{PC})\, G(I_2^{PC}) + q\, F(I_1^{PC}) g(I_2^{PC})(V - I_2^{PC}) \qquad \text{(A.19)}$$
$$+ q\, F(I_1^{PC}) G(I_2^{PC})(-1) = 0.$$

Rearranging yields

$$I_1^{PC} = q \int_{\underline{I}_2}^{I_2^{PC}} (V - I_2)\, g(I_2)\, dI_2 - \frac{F(I_1^{PC})}{f(I_1^{PC})} \tag{A.20}$$

$$I_2^{PC} = V. \tag{A.21}$$

Now consider the second order conditions:

$$\frac{\partial^2 U^{PC}}{\partial I_1^T \partial I_1^T} = -2f(I_1^T) - f'(I_1^T)\left(I_1^T - q\int_{\underline{I}_2}^{I_2{}^T} (V - I_2)\, g(I_2)\, dI_2\right)$$

$$\frac{\partial^2 U^{PC}}{\partial I_2^T \partial I_2^T} = q\left[g'(I_2^T)F(I_1^T)(V - I_2^T) - g(I_2^T)F(I_1^T)\right]$$

$$\frac{\partial^2 U^{PC}}{\partial I_1^T \partial I_2^T} = \frac{\partial^2 U^{PC}}{\partial I_2^T \partial I_1^T} = q\, f(I_1^T)g(I_2^T)(V - I_2^T).$$

At the solutions I_1^{PC} and I_2^{PC}, given by (A.18) and (A.19), $\frac{\partial^2 U^{PC}}{\partial I_1^T \partial I_1^T} = -f(I_1^{PC}) \cdot (1 + H_1'(I_1^{PC})) < 0$. The determinant of the Hessian matrix is given by

$$q\, f(I_1^{PC})g(I_2^{PC})F(I_1^{PC})(1 + H_1'(I_1^{PC})) > 0 \tag{A.22}$$

Therefore the second order conditions are satisfied. □

Proof of Proposition 3.5

The derivatives of the optimal investment threshold I_1^* in the first period with respect to σ_1 and σ_2, respectively, are given by

$$\frac{dI_1^*}{d\sigma_1} = -\frac{1}{2} < 0 \tag{A.23}$$

$$\frac{dI_1^*}{d\sigma_2} = \frac{q}{4}\left[\frac{1}{2} + \frac{1}{2\sigma_2^2}(I_2^* - V)^2\right] > 0$$

□

Proofs for Chapter 4

Proof of Proposition 4.1

First consider the decision at $t = \tau$. If the manager does not switch, residual income in the subsequent periods becomes $RI_t^{ns}(\theta_\tau) = x_{\tau,t} \cdot f_\tau(\theta_\tau)$. Rearranging yields

$$RI_t^{ns}(\theta_\tau) = \frac{x_{\tau,t}}{\sum_{j=\tau+1}^{T} x_{\tau,j}\,\gamma^{j-\tau}} \sum_{j=\tau+1}^{T} x_{\tau t} \cdot f_\tau(\theta_\tau) \cdot \gamma^{j-\tau}$$

If he switches, residual income becomes $RI_t^{s}(\theta_\tau) = x_{\tau,t} \cdot g_\tau(\theta_\tau) - z_{\tau,t} \cdot b_\tau$. Substituting $z_{\tau,t}$ as in (4.6) and rearranging yields

$$RI_t^{s}(\theta_\tau) = \frac{x_{\tau,t}}{\sum_{j=\tau+1}^{T} x_{\tau,j}\,\gamma^{j-\tau}} \left(-b_\tau + \sum_{j=\tau+1}^{T} x_{\tau t} \cdot g_\tau(\theta_\tau) \cdot \gamma^{j-\tau} \right)$$

The manager switches, if and only if his utility from switching is at least as large as his utility, when he keeps the existing product. This condition gives

$$\sum_{t=\tau+1}^{T} \delta^{t-\tau}\, k\, RI_t^{s}(\theta_\tau) \geq \sum_{t=\tau+1}^{T} \delta^{t-\tau}\, k\, RI_t^{ns}(\theta_\tau)$$

Substituting $RI_t^{s}(\theta_\tau)$ and $RI_t^{ns}(\theta_\tau)$ yields

$$\left(-b_\tau + \sum_{j=\tau+1}^{T} x_{\tau t}\, g_\tau(\theta_\tau)\, \gamma^{j-\tau} \right) \sum_{t=\tau+1}^{T} \delta^{t-\tau}\, k \frac{x_{\tau,t}}{\sum_{j=\tau+1}^{T} x_{\tau,j}\,\gamma^{j-\tau}}$$
$$\geq \left(\sum_{j=\tau+1}^{T} x_{\tau t}\, f_\tau(\theta_\tau)\, \gamma^{j-\tau} \right) \sum_{t=\tau+1}^{T} \delta^{t-\tau}\, k \frac{x_{\tau,t}}{\sum_{j=\tau+1}^{T} x_{\tau,j}\,\gamma^{j-\tau}}$$

Dividing by $\sum_{t=\tau+1}^{T} \delta^{t-\tau}\, k \frac{x_{\tau,t}}{\sum_{j=\tau+1}^{T} x_{\tau,j}\,\gamma^{j-\tau}}$ yields headquarters' objective (4.3) for the switching decision. This proves part 3.

Now consider the decision at $t = 0$. If the manager invests, residual income from this decision for each $1 \leq t \leq \tau$ is

$$\begin{aligned} RI_t(\theta_0) &= x_{0,t} \cdot f_0(\theta_0) - z_{0,t} \cdot b_0 \\ &= x_{0,t} \cdot f_0(\theta_0) - \frac{x_{0,t}}{\sum_{j=1}^{T} x_{0,j}\,\gamma^{j}} \cdot b_0 \end{aligned}$$

$$= \frac{x_{0,t}}{\sum_{j=1}^{\tau} x_{0,j}\, \gamma^j} \left(\sum_{j=1}^{\tau} x_{0,j}\, f_0(\theta_0)\, \gamma^j - b_0 \right)$$

$$= \frac{x_{0,t}}{\sum_{j=1}^{\tau} x_{0,j}\, \gamma^j} \left(V_0(\theta_0) - \gamma^\tau \cdot E_{\theta_\tau}[V_\tau(\tilde{\theta}_\tau)] \right)$$

His total utility then becomes

$$\begin{aligned} U(\theta_0) &= \sum_{t=1}^{\tau} \delta^t\, k\, RI_t(\theta_0) \qquad \text{(A.24)} \\ &\quad + \delta^\tau\, E_{\theta_\tau} \left[\max \left\{ \sum_{t=\tau+1}^{T} \delta^{t-\tau}\, k\, RI_t^s(\theta_\tau), \sum_{t=\tau+1}^{T} \delta^{t-\tau}\, k\, RI_t^{ns}(\theta_\tau) \right\} \right] \\ &= \sum_{t=1}^{\tau} \delta^t\, k\, \frac{x_{0,t}}{\sum_{j=1}^{T} x_{0,j}\, \gamma^j} \left(V_0(\theta_0) - \gamma^\tau \cdot E_{\theta_\tau}[V_\tau(\tilde{\theta}_\tau)] \right) \\ &\quad + \delta^\tau \cdot E_{\theta_\tau} [\max\{ \left(-b_\tau + \sum_{j=\tau+1}^{T} x_{\tau,t}\, g_\tau(\tilde{\theta}_\tau)\, \gamma^{j-\tau} \right) \\ &\quad \cdot \sum_{t=\tau+1}^{T} \delta^{t-\tau}\, k\, \frac{x_{\tau,t}}{\sum_{j=\tau+1}^{T} x_{\tau,j}\, \gamma^{j-\tau}}, \\ &\quad \left(\sum_{j=\tau+1}^{T} x_{\tau t}\, f_\tau(\tilde{\theta}_\tau)\, \gamma^{j-\tau} \right) \sum_{t=\tau+1}^{T} \delta^{t-\tau}\, k\, \frac{x_{\tau,t}}{\sum_{j=\tau+1}^{T} x_{\tau,j}\, \gamma^{j-\tau}} \}] \\ &= \sum_{t=1}^{\tau} \delta^t\, k\, \frac{x_{0,t}}{\sum_{j=1}^{T} x_{0,j}\, \gamma^j} \left(V_0(\theta_0) - \gamma^\tau \cdot E_{\theta_\tau}[V_\tau(\tilde{\theta}_\tau)] \right) \\ &\quad + \delta^\tau\, E_{\theta_\tau}[V_\tau(\tilde{\theta}_\tau)] \sum_{t=\tau+1}^{T} \delta^{t-\tau}\, k\, \frac{x_{\tau,t}}{\sum_{j=\tau+1}^{T} x_{\tau,j}\, \gamma^{j-\tau}} \\ &= \sum_{t=1}^{\tau} \delta^t\, k\, \frac{x_{0,t}}{\sum_{j=1}^{T} x_{0,j}\, \gamma^j}\, V_0(\theta_0) \\ &\quad - E_{\theta_\tau}[V_\tau(\tilde{\theta}_\tau)]\, k \left(\gamma^\tau \frac{\sum_{j=1}^{\tau} x_{0,j}\, \delta^j}{\sum_{j=1}^{\tau} x_{0,j}\, \gamma^j} - \delta^\tau \frac{\sum_{j=\tau+1}^{T} x_{\tau,j}\, \delta^{j-\tau}}{\sum_{j=\tau+1}^{T} x_{\tau,j}\, \gamma^{j-\tau}} \right) \end{aligned}$$

If the last term in the manager's utility is 0, his utility would become nonnegative if and only if $V_0(\theta_0) \geq 0$, which is headquarters' objective (4.4). Suppose $\delta = \gamma$. Then the expression in brackets in the last term reduces to 0. In this case residual income is a goal congruent performance measure. If $\delta < \gamma$, in general the expression in brackets is positive. To see this consider the following relation:

$$\gamma^\tau \frac{\sum_{j=1}^{\tau} x_{0,j}\,\delta^j}{\sum_{j=1}^{\tau} x_{0,j}\,\gamma^j} - \delta^\tau \frac{\sum_{j=\tau+1}^{T} x_{\tau,j}\,\delta^{j-\tau}}{\sum_{j=\tau+1}^{T} x_{\tau,j}\,\gamma^{j-\tau}} > \gamma^\tau \frac{\sum_{j=1}^{\tau} x_{0,j}\,\delta^j}{\sum_{j=1}^{\tau} x_{0,j}\,\gamma^j} - \delta^\tau$$

$$= \delta^\tau \left(\frac{\sum_{j=1}^{\tau} x_{0,j}\,\delta^j\,\gamma^\tau}{\sum_{j=1}^{\tau} x_{0,j}\,\gamma^j\,\delta^\tau} - 1 \right) \geq 0$$

The last weak inequality follows from the fact that $\delta^j\,\gamma^\tau/\gamma^j\,\delta^\tau > 1$ for each $j < \tau$ and $\delta^j\,\gamma^\tau/\gamma^j\,\delta^\tau = 1$ for $j = \tau$. Therefore underinvestment occurs if $\delta < \gamma$. □

Proof of Proposition 4.2

First consider the decision at $t = \tau$. In contrast to the previous case, the total amount to be depreciated is increased by Γ_τ. Therefore, residual income in the both cases switching and no switching becomes:

$$RI_t^{ns}(\theta_\tau) = \frac{x_{\tau,t}}{\sum_{j=\tau+1}^{T} x_{\tau,j}\,\gamma^{j-\tau}} \left(-\Gamma_\tau + \sum_{j=\tau+1}^{T} x_{\tau t} \cdot f_\tau(\theta_\tau) \cdot \gamma^{j-\tau} \right)$$

$$RI_t^{s}(\theta_\tau) = \frac{x_{\tau,t}}{\sum_{j=\tau+1}^{T} x_{\tau,j}\,\gamma^{j-\tau}} \left(-b_\tau - \Gamma_\tau + \sum_{j=\tau+1}^{T} x_{\tau t} \cdot g_\tau(\theta_\tau) \cdot \gamma^{j-\tau} \right)$$

Again,the manager switches, if and only if his utility from switching is at least as large as his utility, when he keeps the existing product. Now this condition gives

$$\left(-b_\tau - \Gamma_\tau + \sum_{j=\tau+1}^{T} x_{\tau t}\, g_\tau(\theta_\tau)\,\gamma^{j-\tau} \right) \sum_{t=\tau+1}^{T} \delta^{t-\tau}\, k \frac{x_{\tau,t}}{\sum_{j=\tau+1}^{T} x_{\tau,j}\,\gamma^{j-\tau}}$$

$$\geq \left(-\Gamma_\tau + \sum_{j=\tau+1}^{T} x_{\tau t}\, f_\tau(\theta_\tau)\,\gamma^{j-\tau} \right) \sum_{t=\tau+1}^{T} \delta^{t-\tau}\, k \frac{x_{\tau,t}}{\sum_{j=\tau+1}^{T} x_{\tau,j}\,\gamma^{j-\tau}}$$

This condition yields exactly headquarters' objective (4.3) for the switching decision, independent of the choice of Γ_τ

Now turn to the decision at $t = 0$. The total amount to be depreciated is now lowered by Γ_0. If the manager invests, the residual income from this decision for each $1 \leq t \leq \tau$ is

$$\begin{aligned} RI_t(\theta_0) &= x_{0,t} \cdot f_0(\theta_0) - z_{0,t} \cdot (b_0 - \Gamma_0) \\ &= \frac{x_{0,t}}{\sum_{j=1}^{\tau} x_{0,j}\,\gamma^j} \left(\sum_{j=1}^{\tau} x_{0,j}\, f_0(\theta_0)\,\gamma^j - b_0 + \Gamma_0 \right) \\ &= \frac{x_{0,t}}{\sum_{j=1}^{\tau} x_{0,j}\,\gamma^j} \left(V_0(\theta_0) - \gamma^\tau \cdot E_{\theta_\tau}[V_\tau(\tilde{\theta}_\tau)] + \Gamma_0 \right) \end{aligned}$$

His total utility is

$$
\begin{aligned}
U(\theta_0) = & \sum_{t=1}^{\tau} \delta^t \, k \, RI_t(\theta_0) \\
& + \delta^\tau \, E_{\theta_\tau} \left[\max \left\{ \sum_{t=\tau+1}^{T} \delta^{t-\tau} \, k \, RI_t^s(\tilde{\theta}_\tau), \sum_{t=\tau+1}^{T} \delta^{t-\tau} \, k \, RI_t^{ns}(\tilde{\theta}_\tau) \right\} \right] \\
= & \sum_{t=1}^{\tau} \delta^t \, k \, \frac{x_{0,t}}{\sum_{j=1}^{T} x_{0,j} \, \gamma^j} \left(V_0(\theta_0) - \gamma^\tau \cdot E_{\theta_\tau}[V_\tau(\tilde{\theta}_\tau)] + \Gamma_0 \right) \\
& + \delta^\tau \left(E_{\theta_\tau}[V_\tau(\tilde{\theta}_\tau)] - \Gamma_\tau \right) \sum_{t=\tau+1}^{T} \delta^{t-\tau} \, k \, \frac{x_{\tau,t}}{\sum_{j=\tau+1}^{T} x_{\tau,j} \, \gamma^{j-\tau}}
\end{aligned}
\tag{A.25}
$$

If the parameters Γ_0 and Γ_τ are chosen according to $\Gamma_0 = \gamma^\tau \, E_{\theta_\tau}[V_\tau(\tilde{\theta}_\tau)]$ and $\Gamma_\tau = E_{\theta_\tau}[V_\tau(\tilde{\theta}_\tau)]$, the utility of the manager reduces to

$$
U(\theta_0) = \sum_{t=1}^{\tau} \delta^t \, k \, \frac{x_{0,t}}{\sum_{j=1}^{T} x_{0,j} \, \gamma^j} \, V_0(\theta_0)
$$

Now the managert's utility is positive if and only if headquarters' investment condition (4.4) for the initial investment is satisfied. □

References

M. Amram & N. Kulatilaka (1999). *Real Options. Managing Strategic Investment in an Uncertain World.* Harvard Business School Press, Boston, Massachusetts.

R. M. Anctil & S. Dutta (1999). 'Negotiated Transfer Pricing and Divisional versus Firm-Wide Performance Evaluation'. *The Accounting Review* **74**(1):87–104.

R. N. Anthony & V. Govindarajan (2000). *Management Control Systems.* 10th edition, New York.

R. Antle, et al. (1999). 'Selection from Many Investments with Managerial Private Information'. *Contemporary Accounting Research* **16**(3):397–418.

R. Antle, et al. (2000). *Incentive Problems and Investment Timing Options.* Working Paper.

R. Antle, et al. (2001). 'Information Systems, Incentives and the Timing of Investments'. *Journal of Accounting and Public Policy* **20**:267–294.

R. Antle & G. D. Eppen (1985). 'Capital Rationing and Organizational Slack in Capital Budgeting'. *Management Science* **31**(2):163–174.

R. Antle & J. Fellingham (1990). 'Resource Rationing and Organizational Slack in a Two-Period Model'. *Journal of Accounting Research* **28**(1):1–24.

R. Antle & J. Fellingham (1995). 'Information Rents and Preferences among Information Systems in a Model of Resource Allocation'. *Journal of Accounting Research* **33**:41–58.

R. Antle & J. Fellingham (1997). 'Models of capital investments with private information and incentives: A selective review'. *Journal of Business Finance & Accounting* **24**(7):887–908.

K. J. Arrow (1985). 'The Economics of Agency'. In J. W. Pratt & R. J. Zeckhauser (eds.), *Principals and Agents: The Structure of Business*, pp. 37–51. Harvard Business School Press, Boston.

A. Arya, et al. (1999). *Residual Income, Depreciation, and Empirc Building.* Working Paper.

A. Arya & J. Glover (2001). 'Option Value to Waiting Created by a Control Problem'. *Journal of Accounting Research* **39**(3):405–415.

A. Arya & J. Glover (2002). *Abandonment Options and Information System Design.* Working Paper.

A. Arya, et al. (2001). *Optionality, Decentralization, and Hierarchical Budgeting.* Working Paper.

S. Baiman (1990). 'Agency Research in Managerial Accounting: A Second Look'. *Accounting, Organizations, and Society* **15**(4):341–371.

S. Baiman & M. V. Rajan (1995). 'Centralization, Delegation, and Shared Responsibility in the Assignment of Capital Investment Decision Rights'. *Journal of Accounting Research* **33**:135–164.

T. Baldenius (2002). *Delegated Investment Decisions and Private Benefits of Control.* Working Paper.

T. Baldenius, et al. (1999). 'Zurück zu EVA'. *Betriebswirtschaftliche Forschung und Praxis* **51**(1):53–65.

T. Baldenius, et al. (2002). *Integrating Managerial and Tax Objectives in Transfer Pricing.* Working Paper.

T. Baldenius & S. Reichelstein (2002). *External and Internal Pricing in Multidivisional Firms.* Working Paper.

R. D. Banker & S. M. Datar (1989). 'Sensitivity, Precision, and Linear Aggregation of Signals for Performance Evaluation'. *Journal of Accounting Research* **27**(1):21–39.

R. Benabou & J. Tirole (2002). *Intrinsic and Extrinsic Motivation.* Working Paper.

A. E. Bernardo, et al. (2001). 'Capital budgeting and compensation with asymmetric information and moral hazard'. *Journal of Financial Economics* **61**(3):311–344.

P. Bjerksund & G. Stensland (2000). 'A Self-Enforced Dynamic Contract for Processing of Natural Resources'. In M. J. Brennan & L. Trigeorgis (eds.), *Project Flexibility, Agency, and Competition*, pp. 109–127. New York, Oxford.

F. Black & M. Scholes (1973). 'The Pricing of Options and Corporate Liabilities'. *Journal of Political Economy* **81**:637–654.

R. A. Brealey & S. C. Myers (1996). *Principles of Corporate Finance.* McGraw-Hill, New York et al., 5th ed.

M. J. Brennan & L. Trigeorgis (2000). 'Real Options. Development and New Contributions'. In M. J. Brennan & L. Trigeorgis (eds.), *Project Flexibility, Agency, and Competition*, pp. 1–10. Oxford University Press, New York, Oxford.

M. Bromwich & M. Walker (1998). 'Residual income past and future'. *Management Accounting Research* **9**:391–419.

E. Brousseau & J.-M. Glachant (2002). *The Economics of Contracts.* Cambridge University Press, Cambridge.

J. Budde (2000). *Effizienz betrieblicher Informationssysteme - Vergleich unter Anreizgesichtspunkten.* Wiesbaden.

R. M. Bushman & R. J. Indjejikian (1993). 'Accounting Income, Stock Price, and Managerial Compensation'. *Journal of Accounting and Economics* **16**(1):3–23.

R. M. Bushman, et al. (2000). 'Private Pre-Decision Information, Performance Measure Congruity, and the Value of Delegation'. *Contemporary Accounting Research* **17**:561–587.

W. Busse von Colbe (2002). 'Zur Ermittlung der Kapitalkosten als Bestandteil regulierter Entgelte für Telekommunikationsdienstleistungen'. *zfbf-Sonderheft* **48**:1–25.

J. Butler, et al. (2002). *Intrinsic and Extrinsic Motivation in a Capital Budgeting Setting.* Working Paper.

P. Carr (1988). 'The Valuation of Sequential Exchange Opportunities'. *The Journal of Finance* **43**(5):1235–1256.

P. O. Christensen, et al. (2003). 'Dynamic incentives and responsibility accounting: a comment'. *Journal of Accounting and Economics* **35**(3):423–436.

P. O. Christensen, et al. (2002). '"Cost of capital" in residual income for performance evaluation'. *The Accounting Review* **77**(1):1–23.

T. Copeland & V. Antikarov (2001). *Real Options. A Practitioner's Guide.* New York.

T. E. Copeland & J. F. Weston (1988). *Financial Theory and Corporate Policy.* Addison-Wesley, Reading, Massachusetts et al., 3rd ed.

C. Corona (2002). 'Business Acquisitions and Managerial Performance Evaluation'. Working Paper, Stanford University.

P. Courty & H. Li (2000). 'Sequential Screening'. *Review of Economic Studies* **67**:697–717.

N. Crasselt (2003a). *Accounting-based Investment Incentives and Real Options.* Working Paper.

N. Crasselt (2003b). *Wertorientierte Managemententlohnung, Unternehmensrechnung und Investitionssteuerung.* Peter Lang GmbH, Frankfurt a. Main 2003.

A. Damodaran (2002). *Investment Valuation: Tools and Techniques for Determining the Value of Any Asset.* 2nd edition, John Wiley & Sons.

A. Davila (2003). 'Short-term economic incentives in new product development'. *Research Policy* **32**:1397–1420.

A. K. Dixit & R. S. Pindyck (1994). *Investment under Uncertainty.* Princeton.

S. Dutta (2001). *Managerial Incentives, Investments, and Corporate Growth Options.* Working Paper.

S. Dutta (2003). 'Capital Budgeting and Managerial Compensation: Incentive and Retention Effects'. *The Accounting Review* **78**(1):71–93.

S. Dutta & S. Reichelstein (1999). 'Performance Measurement in Multi-Period Agencies'. *Journal of Institutional and Theoretical Economics* **155**(1):158–175.

S. Dutta & S. Reichelstein (2000). *Stock Price, Earnings and Book Value in Managerial Performance Measures.* Working Paper.

S. Dutta & S. Reichelstein (2002a). *Accrual Accounting for Performance Evaluation: A Synthesis of Recent Proposals.* Working Paper.

S. Dutta & S. Reichelstein (2002b). 'Controlling Investment Decisions: Depreciation- and Capital Charges'. *Review of Accounting Studies* **7**:253–281.

S. Dutta & S. Reichelstein (2002c). *Leading Indicator Variables, Performance Measurement, and Long-Term versus Short-Term Contracts.* Stanford GSB Discussion Paper No 1756.

R. G. Eccles & H. C. White (1988). 'Price and Authority in Inter-Profit center Transactions'. *American Journal of Sociology* **94**:17–51.

D. Egginton (1995). 'Divisional performance measurement: residual income and the asset base'. *Management Accounting Research* **6**:201–222.

A. Ehrbar (1998). *EVA: The Real Key to Creating Wealth.* New York, Chichester.

S. Ekern (1988). 'An Option Pricing Approach to Evaluating Petroleum Projects'. *Energy Economics* **10**:91–99.

R. Ewert & A. Wagenhofer (2003). *Interne Unternehmensrechnung.* 5th edition, Berlin et al.

E. F. Fama (1980). 'Agency Problems and the Theory of the Firm'. *Journal of Political Economy* **88**(2):288–307.

E. F. Fama & M. C. Jensen (1983). 'Separation of Ownership and Control'. *Journal od Law & Economics* **26**(2):301–325.

J. C. Fellingham & R. A. Young (1990). 'The Value of Self-Reported Costs in Repeated Investment Decisions'. *The Accounting Review* **65**(4):837–856.

G. A. Feltham & J. A. Ohlson (1995). 'Valuation and Clean Surplus Accounting for Operating and Financial Activities'. *Contemporary Accounting Research* **11**(2):689–731.

G. A. Feltham & J. Xie (1994). 'Performance Measure Congruity and Diversity in Multi-Task Principal/Agent Relations'. *The Accounting Review* **69**(3):429–453.

E. J. Ferreira & L. Brooks (1988). 'Capital Budgeting: A Key Management Challenge'. *Business* **38**:22–29.

G. Franke & H. Hax (1999). *Finanzwirtschaft des Unternehmens und Kapitalmarkt.* 4th edition, Berlin et al.

J. M. Fremgen (1973). 'Capital Budgeting Practices'. *Management Accounting* **54**(11):19–25.

G. Friedl (2000). *Sequentielle Investitionsentscheidungen unter Unsicherheit.* Duncker & Humblot, Berlin.

G. Friedl (2002a). 'Der Realoptionsansatz zur Bewertung von Investitionen und Akquisitionen'. *M&A Review* (2):93–81.

G. Friedl (2002b). 'Sequential Investment and Time To Build'. *Schmalenbach Business Review* **54**(1):58–79.

D. Fudenberg & J. Tirole (1992). *Game Theory.* The MIT Press, Cambridge, Massachusetts, London, England.

R. Gibbons (1998). 'Incentives in Organizations'. *Journal of Economic Perspectives* **12**(4):115–132.

R. M. Gillenkirch & M. M. Schabel (2001). 'Investitionssteuerung, Motivation und Periodenerfolgsrechnung bei ungleichen Zeitpräferenzen'. *zfbf* **53**(3):216–245.

L. J. Gitman & J. R. Forrester Jr. (1977). 'A Survey of Capital Budgeting Techniques Used by Major U.S. Firms'. *Financial Management* **6**(3):66–71.

C. D. Green, et al. (2002). 'A Possible Economic Rationale for Straight-Line Depreciation'. *Abacus* **38**(1):91–120.

S. R. Grenadier (1996). 'The Strategic Exercise of Options: Development Cascades and Overbuilding in Real Estate Markets'. *The Journal of Finance* **51**(5):1653–1679.

S. R. Grenadier & N. Wang (2003). *Incentives and Investment Timing: Real Options in a Principal-Agent Setting.* Working Paper, Stanford University.

S. Grossman & O. Hart (1983). 'An Analysis of the Principal-Agent Problem'. *Econometrica* **51**:7–45.

T. M. Groves (1973). 'Incentives in Teams'. *Econometrica* pp. 617–631.

T. M. Groves & M. Loeb (1979). 'Incentives in a Divisionalized Firm'. *Management Science* **25**(3):221–230.

R. F. Göx (2000). 'Strategic Transfer Pricing, Absorption Costing, and Observability'. *Management Accounting Research* **11**(3):327–348.

D. Hachmeister (2002). 'Erfolgsorientierte PerformancemaSSe'. In H.-U. Küpper & A. Wagenhofer (eds.), *Handwörterbuch Unternehmensrechnung und Controlling*, pp. 1385–1395. Schäffer-Poeschel, Stuttgart, 4 edn.

D. R. Hansen & M. M. Mowen (2000). *Management Accounting.* South-Western College Publishing, Cincinnati, Ohio.

M. Harris, et al. (1982). 'Asymmetric Information, Incentives, and Intrafirm Resource Allocation'. *Management Science* **28**(6):604–620.

M. Harris & A. Raviv (1996). 'The Capital Budeting Process: Incentives and Information'. *The Journal of Finance* **51**(4):1139–1174.

M. Harris & A. Raviv (1998). 'Capital budgeting and delegation'. *Journal of Financial Economics* **50**:259–289.

M. Harris & R. M. Townsend (1981). 'Resource Allocation under Asymmetric Information'. *Econometrica* **49**(1):33–64.

A. G. Hart (1940). *Anticipations, Uncertainty, and Dynamic Planning.* New York.

O. Hart & B. Holmström (1987). 'The Theory of Contracts'. In T. Bewley (ed.), *Advances in Economic Theory*, pp. 37–51. Cambridge University Press, Cambridge.

H. Hax (1989). 'Investitionsrechnung und Periodenerfolgsmessung'. In W. Delfmann (ed.), *Der Integrationsgedanke in der Betriebswirtschaftslehre*, pp. 154–170. Wiesbaden.

H. Hax & H. Laux (1972). 'Flexible Planung - Verfahrensregeln und Entscheidungsmodelle für die Planung bei UngewiSSheit'. *zfbf* **24**:318–340.

M. Hebertinger (2001). *WertsteigerungsmaSSe - eine kritische Analyse.* Verlag Peter Lang, Frankfurt am Main et al.

R. W. Hilton, et al. (2000). *Cost Management: Strategies for Business Decisions.* McGraw-Hill, New York.

C. Hofmann (2001). *Anreizorientierte Controllingsysteme.* Schäffer-Poeschel Verlag, Stuttgart.

B. Holmström (1979). 'Moral Hazard and Observability'. *Bell Journal of Economics* **10**:74–91.

B. Holmström & P. Milgrom (1987). 'Aggregation and Linearity in the Provision of Intertemporal Incentives'. *Econometrica* **55**(2):303–328.

B. Holmström & L. Weiss (1985). 'Managerial Incentives, Investment and Aggregate Implications: Scale Effects'. *Review of Economic Studies* pp. 403–425.

U. Hommel, et al. (2003). *Reale Optionen. Konzepte, Praxis und Perspektiven strategischer Unternehmensfinanzierung.* Berlin et al.

C. T. Horngren, et al. (1999). *Management and Cost Accounting.* Prentice Hall Europe, London et al. 1999.

C. T. Horngren & G. Foster (1991). *Cost Accounting - A Managerial Emphasis.* Prentice Hall International Editions, Englewood Cliffs, NJ.

S. Hostettler (1997). *Economic Value Added.* 2nd ed., Bern et al.

Y. Hu & O. Bernt (1998). 'Optimal time to invest when the price processes are geometric Brownian motions'. *Finance and Stochastics* **2**(3):295–310.

R. Indjejikian & D. Nanda (1999). 'Dynamic incentives and responsibility accounting'. *Journal of Accounting and Economics* **27**(2):177–201.

J. E. Ingersoll jr. & S. Ross (1992). 'Waiting to Invest: Investment and Uncertainty'. *Journal of Business* **65**(1):2–29.

M. C. Jensen (2001). 'Corporate Budgeting is Broken: Let's Fix It'. *Harvard Business Review* pp. 94–101.

M. C. Jensen & W. H. Meckling (1976). 'Theory of the Firm: Managerial Behavior, Agency Costs and Ownership Structure'. *Journal of Financial Economics* **3**:305–360.

I. Jewitt (1988). 'Justifying the First-Order Approach to Principal-Agent Problems'. *Econometrica* **56**:1177–1190.

P.-J. Jost (2001a). 'Die Prinzipal-Agenten-Theorie im Unternehmenskontext'. In P.-J. Jost (ed.), *Die Prinzipal-Agenten-Theorie in der Betriebswirtschaftslehre*, pp. 11–43. Schäffer-Poeschel, Stuttgart.

P.-J. Jost (2001b). *Die Prinzipal-Agenten-Theorie in der Betriebswirtschaftslehre.* Stuttgart.

C. W. Kester (1984). 'Today's Options for Tomorrow's Growth'. *Harvard Business Review* **62**:153–160.

C. W. Kester (1993). 'Turning Growth Options Into Real Assets'. In R. Aggarwal (ed.), *Capital Budgeting Under Uncertainty*, pp. 187–207. Englewood Cliffs.

W. C. Kester & R. A. Taggart Jr. (1989). 'Capital Allocation - Hurdle Rates, Budgets, or Both?'. *MIT Sloan Management Review* **30**(3):83–90.

A. J. Kirby, et al. (1991). 'Participation, Slack, and Budget Based Performance Evaluation'. *Journal of Accounting Research* **29**(1):109–128.

H.-U. Küpper (1998). 'Marktwertorientierung - neue und realisierbare Ausrichtung für die interne Unternehmensrechnung?'. *Betriebswirtschaftliche Forschung und Praxis* (5):517–539.

H.-U. Küpper (2001). *Controlling. Konzeption, Aufgaben und Instrumente.* 3rd ed., Stuttgart.

H.-U. Küpper (2002). 'Kostenorientierte Preisbestimmung für regulierte Märkte - Analyse eines Beispiels der Bedeutung betriebswirtschaftlicher Begriffe und Konzepte'. *zfbf-Sonderheft* **48**:27–55.

D. M. Kreps (1997). 'The Interaction Between Norms and Economic Incentives: Intrinsic Motivation and Extrinsic Incentives'. *American Economic Review, Papers and Proceedings* **87**:359–364.

J.-J. Laffont & D. Martimort (2002). *The Theory of Incentives. The Principal-Agent Model.* Princeton University Press, Princeton, Oxford.

J.-J. Laffont & J. Tirole (1986). 'Using Cost Observation to Regulate Firms'. *The Journal of Political Economy* **94**(3):614–641.

J.-J. Laffont & J. Tirole (1988). 'The Dynamics of Incentive Contracts'. *Econometrica* **56**(5):1153–1175.

J.-J. Laffont & J. Tirole (1993). *A Theory of Incentives in Procurement and Regulation.* Cambridge, Massachusetts.

R. A. Lambert (1986). 'Executive Effort and Selection of Risky Projects'. *The Rand Journal of Economics* **17**(1):77–88.

R. A. Lambert (2001). 'Contracting theory and accounting'. *Journal of Accounting and Economics* **32**:3–87.

C. Laux (2001). 'Limited Liability and Incentive Contracting with Multiple Projects'. *Rand Journal of Economics* **32**(3):514–526.

H. Laux (1971). *Flexible Investitionsplanung. Einführung in die Theorie der sequentiellen Entscheidungen bei Unsicherheit.* Opladen.

H. Laux (1995). *Erfolgssteuerung und Organisation 1. Anreizkompatible Erfolgsrechnung, Erfolgsbeteiligung und Erfolgskontrolle.* Berlin et al.

H. Laux (1999). *Unternehmensrechnung, Anreiz und Kontrolle.* Springer Verlag, Berlin et al.

W. Lücke (1955). 'Investitionsrechnungen auf der Grundlage von Ausgaben oder Kosten'. *zfbf* **7**:310–324.

J. Lorie & L. Savage (1955). 'Three Problems in Capital Rationing'. *Journal of Business* pp. 228–39.

D. G. Luenberger (1998). *Investment Science.* Oxford University Press, New York, Oxford.

J. F. Magee (1964). 'How to Use Decision Trees in Capital Investment'. *Harvard Business Review* **42**:79–96.

W. Margrabe (1978). 'The Value of an Option to Exchange One Asset for Another'. *The Journal of Finance* **33**:177–186.

E. Matson (1999). 'Capital rationing'. *Scandinavian Journal of Management* **15**(2):157–171.

R. McDonald & D. Siegel (1986). 'The Value of Waiting to Invest'. *The Quarterly Journal of Economics* **101**:707–727.

H. Meinhövel (1999). *Defizite der Principal-Agent-Theorie.* Josef Eul Verlag, Lohmar, Köln.

N. D. Melumad & S. Reichelstein (1987). 'Centralization versus Delegation and the Value of Communication'. *Journal of Accounting Research (Supplement)* **25**:1–18.

R. C. Merton (1973). 'Theory of Rational Option Pricing'. *The Bell Journal of Economics and Management Science* **4**(1):141–183.

P. Milgrom & J. Roberts (1992). *Economics, Organization and Management.* Prentice Hall, Upper Saddle River, NJ.

J. Mirrlees (1999). 'The Theory of Moral Hazard and Unobservable Behaviour: Part I'. *Review of Economic Studies* **66**:3–21.

B. Mittendorf (2003). *Information Revelation, Incentives, and the Value of a Real Option.* Working Paper.

S. Myers (1977). 'Determinants of Corporate Borrowing'. *Journal of Financial Economics* **5**:147–175.

R. B. Myerson (1979). 'Incentive Compatibility and the Bargaining Problem'. *Econometrica* **47**(1):61–73.

D. V. Neher (1999). 'Staged Financing: An Agency Perspective'. *Review of Economic Studies* **66**:255–274.

O. Neuberger (1980). 'Motivation'. In E. Grochla (ed.), *Handwörterbuch der Organisation*, pp. 1356–1365. C. E. Poeschel, Stuttgart, 2 edn.

J. O'Hanlon & K. Peasnell (1998). 'Wall Street's contribution to management accounting: the Stern Stewart EVA financial management system'. *Management Accounting Research* **9**:421–444.

J. A. Ohlson (1995). 'Earnings, Book Values, and Dividends in Equity Valuation'. *Contemporary Accounting Research* **11**(2):661–687.

K. Osband & S. Reichelstein (1985). 'Information-Eliciting Compensation Schemes'. *Journal of Public Economics* **27**:107–115.

J. L. Paddock, et al. (1988). 'Option Valuation of Claims on Real Assets: The Case of Offshore Petroleum Leases'. *The Quarterly Journal of Economics* **103**:479–508.

B. Pedell (2003). *Festlegung der Kapitalkostenbasis für Zwecke der Entgeltregulierung.* Working Paper.

B. Pellens, et al. (1998). 'Wertorientierte Entlohnungssysteme für Führungskräfte - Anforderungen und empirische Evidenz'. In B. Pellens (ed.), *Unternehmenswertorientierte Entlohnungssysteme*, pp. 1–28. Stuttgart.

J. W. Petty, et al. (1975). 'The Capital Expenditure Decision-Making Process of Large Corporations'. *The Engineering Economist* pp. 159–172.

D. Pfaff (1998). 'Wertorientierte Unternehmenssteuerung, Investitionsentscheidungen und Anreizprobleme'. *Betriebswirtschaftliche Forschung und Praxis* **50**(5):491–516.

T. Pfeiffer (2000). 'Good and Bad News for the Implementation of Shareholder-Value Concepts in Decentralized Organizations'. *Schmalenbach Business Review* **52**:68–91.

T. Pfeiffer (2002). 'Kostenbasierte oder verhandlungsorientierte Verrechnungspreise? Weiterführende Überlegungen zur Leistungsfähigkeit der Verfahren'. *ZfB* **72**(12):1269–1291.

T. Pfeiffer (2003). 'Anreizkompatible Unternehmenssteuerung, Performancemasse und Erfolgsrechnung - Zur Vorteilhaftigkeit von Ergebnisgrössen bei unbekannten Zeitpräferenzen des Managers'. *Die Betriebswirtschaft* **63**(1):43–59.

J. M. Poterba & L. H. Summers (1995). 'A CEO Survey of U.S. Companies' Time Horizons and Hurdle Rates'. *MIT Sloan Management Review* **37**(1):43–53.

G. A. D. Preinreich (1937). 'Valuation and Amortization'. *The Accounting Review* **12**:209–226.

J. S. Reece & W. R. Cool (1982). 'Measuring Investment Center Performance'. In A. Rappaport (ed.), *Information for Decision Making*, pp. 264–277. Prentice Hall, Englewood Cliffs, 3 edn.

S. Reichelstein (1992). 'Constructing Incentive Schemes for Governement Contracts: An application of Agency Theory'. *The Accounting Review* **67**(4):712–731.

S. Reichelstein (1997). 'Investment Decisions and Managerial Performance Evaluation'. *Review of Accounting Studies* **2**:157–180.

S. Reichelstein (2000). 'Providing managerial incentives: Cash flows versus accrual accounting'. *Journal of Accounting Research* **38**:243–270.

C. Riegler (2000). *Hierarchische Anreizsysteme im wertorientierten Management: eine agencytheoretische Untersuchung.* Stuttgart.

W. P. Rogerson (1985). 'The First-Order Approach to Principal-Agent Problems'. *Econometrica* **53**:1357–1367.

W. P. Rogerson (1997). 'Intertemporal Cost Allocation and Managerial Investment Incentives: A Theory Explaining the Use of Economic Value Added as a Performance Measure'. *Journal of Political Economy* **105**(4):770–795.

M. Ross (1986). 'Capital Budgeting Practices of Twelve Large Manufacturers'. *Financial Management* **15**(4):15–22.

B. Rudolph (1986). 'Neuere Kapitalkostenkonzepte auf der Grundlage der Kapitalmarkttheorie'. *zfbf* **38**(10):892–898.

P. A. Ryan & G. P. Ryan (2002). 'Capital Budgeting Practices of the Fortune 1000: How Have Things Changed'. *The Journal of Business and Management* **8**(4):355–364.

D. Sappington (1983). 'Limited Liability Contracts between Principal and Agent'. *Journal of Economic Theory* **29**:1–21.

U. Schiller (2001). *Decentralized Information Acquisition and the Internal Provision of Capital.* Working Paper, University of Tuebingen.

R. H. Schmidt (1990). *Grundzüge der Investitions- und Finanzierungstheorie.* 2nd ed., Wiesbaden.

D. Sliwka (2002). 'On the Use of Nonfinancial Performance Measures in Management Compensation'. *Journal of Economics and Management Strategy* **11**:487–511.

H. T. J. Smit (1997). 'Investment Analysis of Offshore Concessions in the Netherlands'. *Financial Management* **26**(2):5–17.

D. Solomons (1965). *Divisional Performance: Measurement and Control.* Homewood, Illinois.

K. Spremann (1987). 'Agent and Principal'. In G. Bamberg & K. Spremann (eds.), *Agency Theory, Information, and Incentives*, pp. 3–37. Springer, Berlin et al.

M. T. Stanley & S. B. Block (1984). 'A Survey of Multinational Capital Budgeting'. *Financial Review* **19**:36–54.

A. W. Stark (2000). 'Real Options, (Dis)Investment Decision-Making and Accounting Measures of Performance'. *Journal of Business Finance & Accounting* **27**(3):313–331.

J. M. Stern, et al. (2001). *The EVA Challenge - Implementing Value-Added Change in an Organization.* Wiley, New York et al.

G. B. Stewart III (1991). *The Quest for Value.* New York.

R. A. Taggart Jr. (1987). 'Allocating Capital among a Firm's Divisions: Hurdle Rates vs. Budgets'. *Journal of Financial Research* pp. 177–189.

V. Trauzettel (1999). *Dynamische Koordinationsmechanismen für das Controlling.* Berlin.

L. Trigeorgis (1996). *Real Options. Managerial Flexibility and Strategy in Resource Allocation.* Cambridge, Massachusetts.

L. J. Velthuis (2003). 'Managemententlohnung auf Basis des Residualgewinns: Theoretische Anforderungen und praxisrelevante Konzepte'. *ZfB-Ergänzungsheft* (4):111–135.

A. Wagenhofer (2002). 'Verrechnungspreise'. In H.-U. Küpper & A. Wagenhofer (eds.), *Handwörterbuch Unternehmensrechnung und Controlling*, pp. 2074–2083. Schäffer-Poeschel, Stuttgart, 4 edn.

A. Wagenhofer (2003). 'Accrual-based compensation, depreciation and investment decisions'. *European Accounting Review* **12**(2):287–309.

A. Wagenhofer & R. Ewert (1993). 'Linearität und Optimalität in ökonomischen Agency-Modellen - Zur Rechtfertigung des LEN- Modells'. *Zeitschrift für Betriebswirtschaft* **63**(4):373–391.

A. Wagenhofer & C. Riegler (1999). 'Gewinnabhängige Managemententlohnung und Investitionsanreize'. *Betriebswirtschaftliche Forschung und Praxis* **51**(1):70–90.

M. H. Weingartner (1977). 'Capital Rationing: n authors in search of a plot'. *Journal of Finance* **32**:1403–1432.

M. L. Weitzman (1976). 'The New Soviet Incentive Model'. *Bell Journal of Economics* **7**(1):251–257.

R. B. Wilson (1969). 'Investment Analysis Under Uncertainty'. *Management Science* **15**(12):650–664.

S. D. Young & S. F. O'Byrne (2001). *EVA and Value-Based Management: A Practical Guide to Implementation.* New York.

G. Zhang (1997). 'Moral Hazard in Corporate Investment and the Disciplinary Role of Voluntary Capital Rationing'. *Management Science* **43**(6):737–750.

Printing: Krips bv, Meppel
Binding: Stürtz, Würzburg